Divine Reflections

in Times and Seasons

Eva Peck

© 2013 by Eva Peck

All rights reserved

Except for any fair dealing permitted under the Copyright Act, no part of this book may be reproduced by any means without prior permission of the author and publisher.

Photography: Alexander Peck with the exception of
Pages 23 (left), which is the credit of Eva Peck
Page 75, which is courtesy of www.freedigitalphotos.net
Page 104, which is the credit of Jindrich Degen

Graphic design and cover design: Eva Peck

Bible quotes and paraphrases taken from the HOLY BIBLE, NEW INTERNATIONAL VERSION. Copyright © 1973, 1978, 1984 by International Bible Society. Used by permission of Zondervan Publishing House. All rights reserved.

National Library of Australia Cataloguing-in-Publication entry

Author: Peck, Eva.
Title: Divine reflections in times and seasons / Eva Peck; Alexander Peck, photographer.

ISBN: 9780987090584 (pbk.)

Subjects: Seasons--Religious aspects.
Nature--Religious aspects.
Spiritual formation.
Spiritual life.

Other Authors/Contributors: Peck, Alexander.

Dewey Number: 248.2

The book can be purchased online through:
www.heavens-reflections.org or www.pathway-publishing.org

Pathway Publishing
Seeking truth and beauty

Dedicated to the Creator God
and all lovers of nature.

Other Books by the Same Author

Divine Reflections in Natural Phenomena

Divine Reflections in Living Things

Divine Insights from Human Life

Co-author of:

Pathway to Life – Through the Holy Scriptures

Journey to the Divine Within – Through Silence, Stillness and Simplicity

Acknowledgments

First, I would like to thank the Great God for enabling, inspiring and blessing this small publication.

I must also thank my husband, Alex, for his encouragement and support. He is always ready to help with editing and to give helpful advice. Without his valuable input, this book would not have come out as it has.

Contents

Preface 9

Introduction 14
  Insights from Writers and Poets 15
  Implications 19
  Appreciate the Divine Beauty 20

All in a Day 23
  Light and Vision 25
  Darkness and Blindness 30
  Different Views of Life 36

All in a Week 40
  Weekly Rest Day in History and the Bible 42
  Seven-Day Cycles in the Bible 43
  Sabbath as a Rest Day 44
  Spiritual Realities Depicted by the Sabbath 46

All in a Month 49
  Lunar Phases and Life Cycles 49
  Moon Phases in Biblical Israel 51

All in a Year 56
  Seasons of the Year 58
  Spring 59
  Summer 61
  Autumn 62
  Winter 63
  Seasonal Celebrations in Ancient Israel 64
  Paradise – Old and New 66

Little by Little 68
- Universal Law of Gradual Change 68
- Gentle Working of the Divine........................... 70
- When Little by Little Doesn't Work 73

Turning Points 75
- Turning Points in Biblical History 77
- Upcoming Turning Points 80

Time for Everything 83
- Time-Based Universe 84
- Sovereign Time Master 87

In the Nick of Time 90
- Critical Timing in Nature 91
- Last-Minute Divine Intervention 92
- When God Doesn't Intervene 94

Strangers in Time.. 96
- Divinity in Time.. 97
- Longing to Transcend Time 99
- On a Journey to Eternity 100

About the Author 104

More About the Author's Other Books 106

Other Resources 108

Readers' Comments 110

About Pathway Publishing 113

Preface

I have loved and been interested in nature since childhood. Growing up in Central Europe, I would see our small backyard garden transform during each of the four seasons. In the spring, I watched the first crocus flowers break through the cold soil. Then came the tulip leaves and peony shoots. Before long, the tulips, peonies, pansies, and fruit trees were all in bloom. As the year progressed, the garden continually changed. Early in the summer we picked cherries, then apricots. Later came the apples and pears. By late autumn, the flowering plants dried up, the leaves fell off the trees, and the whole garden went into hibernation to again awaken in the spring.

During various times of the year, family trips to the woods, meadows and mountains always spoke to my heart. I admired carpets of violets and anemones on the ground, pine trees towering in the air, interestingly shaped cones sometimes having been nibbled by a hungry squirrel, the various kinds of mushrooms ranging from shades of brown to bright red, ferns by the side of a gurgling stream, fish and tadpoles in the water, and much more.

There were beetles and butterflies of various colours and sizes, pink earthworms and hairy caterpillars, hares and deer almost always on the run, birds such as pheasants or woodpeckers, mice and other rodents scampering into their holes, and even an occasional snake. I would pick up cones, bird feathers, flowers, and coloured autumn leaves. We also feasted on blueberries, strawberries, raspberries, and blackberries. My parents taught me the names of the many living things that we encountered on our nature walks. I knew which mushrooms were edible and which snakes were dangerous. In winter, a blanket of shimmering snow on sunlit forest trees provided a different kind of atmosphere, but no less inspiring.

While nature has always spoken to me, and my interest in it later led me to study science in high school and university, God as the Creator or the Mind behind all that exists was not a part of my consciousness as a child. It was only in my late teens that I was led to start reading the Bible. At that time, it was again nature that confirmed to me God's existence. The analogies of a watch having to have a watchmaker, laws having to be made by a law giver, and design requiring a designer made perfect sense as I continued to study both the Holy Scriptures and nature.

As time went on, I became well acquainted with the message of the Bible and the divine plan it reveals for humanity. Then I began to see nature and many daily occurrences as a mirror of the spiritual realities portrayed in the Scriptures. This became the genesis of this book, the first of a trilogy. The two sequels are *Divine Reflections in Natural Phenomena* and *Divine Reflections in Living Things*.

Divine Reflections in Times and Seasons aims to inspire a fresh look at the physical world and life around us – to see each sunrise, sunset, moon phase, season change, and even the passage of time itself in a new way. The writer of Psalm 19 and other biblical authors point us to the natural world to perceive divine glories. For those who pause and take time to see and ponder, there is a continuous, abundant, and universal revelation of God. The divine nature is perceivable in the starry heavens as well as in life on the earth. The physical creation is a divine vehicle to demonstrate in a way we can comprehend and that transcends all languages perfect love, wisdom, power, and other divine qualities.

The Psalmist describes the skies as "the work of God's hands" (19:1). When we see nature as God's creation, we can infer it is sacred and therefore needs to be respected. With properly esteeming and caring for nature, many man-made environmental problems would not exist – in place of abuse and exploitation of the earth and its resources, there would be a new-found awe, praise, and gratitude. Just as we can always see something of the artist in his or her creative works, we can see a reflection of the Divine in nature.

Preface

The earth and physical universe speak the praises of God through their beauty, complexity, balance, order, and even through the mindboggling size of the cosmos.

While this book is based on the assumption that God or a Higher Power is behind all that exists, I do not insist on the literal interpretation of all biblical accounts, as I have come to understand that the Scriptures are not intended to be a strictly scientific or historical work. The assumption is, however, that biblical accounts reveal, sometimes in symbolic language, God's deeds in human history and also point to unseen spiritual realities. Often poetry and metaphor are the best or only vehicles to communicate what is inexpressible in literal language.

I understand that the Divine is neither male nor female. However, to use the pronoun "it" seems inappropriate, therefore I am opting for the grammatical gender "he".

For those who would like to learn more about the biblical teachings behind the observations, the footnotes provide scriptural references for the conclusions reached.

The idea that the physical world pictures spiritual realities is neither new nor unique to this book. However, each writer who has ever expressed this thought has done it in a unique way based on their own inspiration and experience. Here are my perceptions and understanding of how certain natural occurrences can be viewed in spiritual terms. May it give you new insights and a different perspective as you take a fresh look at the daily aspects of your life.

Eva Peck

Introduction

"But ask the animals, and they will teach you,
or the birds of the air, and they will tell you;
or speak to the earth, and it will teach you,
or let the fish of the sea inform you.
Which of all these does not know
that the hand of the LORD has done this?
In his hand is the life of every creature and the breath of all mankind."
(Job 12:7-10)

The Bible points us to the natural world around us – the living things as well as the heavens and the earth to learn about God. Psalm 19:1-4 states: "The heavens declare the glory of God; the skies proclaim the work of his hands. Day after day they pour forth speech; night after night they display knowledge. There is no speech or language where their voice is not heard. Their voice goes out into all the earth, their words to the ends of the world."

Everywhere we look, if we take but a moment to try to see in a fresh way, nature speaks of divine qualities. "What may be known about God is plain to them, because God has made it plain to them. For since the creation of the world God's invisible qualities – his eternal power and divine nature – have been clearly seen, being understood from what has been made" (Romans 1:19-20).

Over the centuries, thinkers and philosophers have caught glimpses of the divine in the natural world. In fact, a branch of Christian theology is called Natural Theology. Its basic tenets are that God has revealed himself both naturally and supernaturally. The European thinker and theologian, Jan Amos Comenius (1592-1670), called nature "The Living Book of God" and the Bible "The Living Word of God." As mentioned, the Scriptures affirm that divine attributes may be known from what exists because the creation points towards its Creator. Truths about God that can be learned from nature, humanity, and the world around us include God's existence and divine qualities such as love, intelligence, design, order and harmony. This knowledge is then complemented and enriched by supernaturally revealed information, such as about grace and salvation. There is a continuum between that which can be understood by the natural light of human reason and that which is received by the light of faith.

Insights from Writers and Poets

Various writers and poets have also mused about the divine in the natural order and we can gain insights and inspiration from their thoughts. Consider, for example, what Victorian poet, *Elizabeth Barrett Browning* saw in nature:

> Earth is crammed with heaven,
> And every common bush afire with God,
> But only he who sees takes off his shoes;
> The rest sit round it and pluck blackberries.

Gerard Manley Hopkins, nineteenth-century priest and poet insisted that "The world is charged with the grandeur of God."

Reformation theologian *John Calvin* wrote: "[God's] nature is incomprehensible, far beyond all human thought, but his glory is etched on his creation so brightly, clearly, and gloriously that no one however obtuse and illiterate can plead ignorance as an excuse.... Wherever you look, there is no part of the world however small that does not show at least some glimmer of beauty; it is impossible to gaze at the vast expanse of the universe without being overwhelmed by such tremendous beauty. So the author of the epistle to the Hebrews sensitively describes the visible world as an image of the invisible (Hebrews 11:3)."

Calvin also stated: "When a man, from beholding and contemplating the heavens, has been brought to acknowledge God, he will learn also to reflect upon and to admire his wisdom and power as displayed on the face of the earth, not only in general, but even in the minutest of plants."

Henry David Thoreau (1817 - 1862), American transcendentalist who spent two years living in a small cabin near a pond in the woods remarked: "Blessed are they who never read a newspaper, they shall see nature, and through her, God."

English poet *William Blake* (1757 -1827) perceived eternity in every cell: "And every space smaller than a globule of man's blood opens into Eternity of which this vegetable Earth is but a shadow."

Russian writer *Fyodor Dostoyevsky* (1821-1881) wrote in his famous novel, *The Brothers Karamazov*: "Every blade of grass, every insect, ant, and golden bee, all so marvellously know their path; though they have not intelligence, they bear witness to the mystery of God and continually accomplish it themselves." Through one of his characters, Dostoyevsky also exhorts: "Love all of God's creation, the whole of it and every grain of sand. Love every leaf, every ray of God's light! Love the animals. Love the plants, love everything. If you love everything, you will soon perceive the divine mystery in things. Once you perceive it, you will begin to comprehend it better every day. And you will come at last to love the whole world with an all-embracing love."

A more contemporary spiritual writer, *Henri Nouwen* (1932-1996), shares the following: "When God took on flesh in Jesus Christ, the uncreated and the created, the eternal and the temporal, the divine and the human became united. This unity meant that all that is mortal now points to the immortal, all that is finite now points to the infinite. In and through Jesus all creation has become like a splendid veil, through which the face of God is revealed to us. This is called the sacramental quality of the created order. All that is is sacred because all that is speaks of God's redeeming love. Seas and winds, mountains and trees, sun, moon, and stars, and all the animals and people have become sacred windows offering us glimpses of God."

Physicist *Albert Einstein*, although not a Christian believer, perceived God in the wonders of the universe. When asked by an interviewer if he was an atheist, he replied: "I'm not an atheist. The problem involved is too vast for our limited minds. We are in the position of a little child entering a huge library filled with books in many languages. The child knows someone must have written those books. It does not know how. It does not understand the languages in which they are written. The child dimly suspects a mysterious order in the arrangement of the books but doesn't know what it is. That, it seems to me, is the attitude of even the most intelligent human being toward God. We see the universe marvellously arranged and obeying certain laws but only dimly understand these laws."

Implications

Seeing divinity all around us calls for a response. *C. S. Lewis* expressed it as follows: "Because God created the Natural – invented it out of his love and artistry – it demands our reverence."

Nouwen asked and answered: "How do we live in creation? Do we relate to it as a place full of 'things' we can use for whatever need we want to fulfil and whatever goal we wish to accomplish? Or do we see creation first of all as a sacramental reality, a sacred space where God reveals to us the immense beauty of the Divine? As long as we only use creation, we cannot recognize its sacredness because we are approaching it as if we are its owners. But when we relate to all that surrounds us as created by the same God who created us and as the place where God appears to us and calls us to worship and adoration, then we are able to recognize the sacred quality of all God's handiwork."

Dean Ohlman, Christian writer and advocate for environmental responsibility, challenges us: "Creation speaks of the Creator. Are you listening? When you are faced with the grandeur, power, and beauty of creation, does your vision linger there or do you follow the sign to the object? Are you nearsighted, focusing solely on the beauty in front of you instead of on the God behind the beauty? And when you do see Him, how do you respond? Consider Psalm 104: After writing 32 verses celebrating the work of our Creator, the psalmist gives us his response: 'I will sing to the Lord as long as I live; I will sing praise to my God while I have my being. May my meditation be sweet to Him; I will be glad in the Lord.' (Psalm 104:33)."

German theologian *Jürgen Moltmann* sums it up: "For centuries, men and women have tried to understand God's creation as nature, so that they can exploit it in accordance with the laws science has discovered. Today the essential point is to understand this knowable, controllable, and usable nature as God's creation, and to learn to respect it as such."

Appreciate the Divine Beauty

Our often insensitive and utilitarian approach to the natural world is a result of the loss of a theology of beauty – the recognition that the beauty in the natural world is one of the most important evidences of God's divine nature.

Nineteenth century American statesman *George Bancroft* expressed it like this: "Beauty is but the sensible image of the Infinite. Like truth and justice it lives within us; like virtue and the moral law it is a companion of the soul."

Introduction

Naturalist, writer and conservationist *John Muir* believed that "everybody needs beauty as well as bread, places to play in and pray in where nature may heal and cheer and give strength to body and soul alike."

The value of natural beauty to the human soul was what inspired the masterful landscape painter *Thomas Cole*, founder of the Hudson River School of painting. With his paintings he wanted to put people back in touch with the Creator. He hoped his paintings would give city-dwelling admirers a yearning for the outdoors where they too could discover what he had – that "in gazing on the pure creations of the Almighty, [one] feels a calm religious tone steal through [the] mind, and when [one] has turned to mingle [again] with [one's] fellow [humans], the chords which have been struck in that sweet communion cease not to vibrate."

The unfathomable reality and divine purpose is far larger than our minds can surmise. But perhaps it can be imagined as a giant hologram wherein each part contains the whole. No matter into how many parts a holograph is subdivided, the same picture remains. After a great many cuts in half, the holograph begins to get a little fuzzy, as it loses some of its detail, but the entire picture is still there. The chapters in this book therefore take a deeper look at various everyday aspects of physical realities to see what can be glimpsed of the total picture. It then draws from what we see, based on the Bible, lessons for physical and spiritual life.

You are invited to come and read both the Book of God and the Word of God and see what treasures may be found there as far as God's character and the divine plan for humanity. Try to break away and spend some time in nature – noticing the sunlight on the trees and flowers, the growth and unfolding of new leaves, the variety of creatures that cross your path. Take a fresh look at the sea and the dry land, the birds and the bees, the sky and clouds, as well as the starry heavens.

May such a new look at things we take for granted bring us to a sense of wonder, awe, and gratitude at the marvels around us. May we come to recognize the sacred and divine in all things and begin to feel at one with God and all of creation.

All in a Day

The dark blue in the western sky contrasted with the light blue toward the east. The morning star, as well as a new moon, was still visible, but so were contours of palms, bushes, and rock formations. Another day in the desert was breaking in a glorious way. Little by little, almost imperceptibly, more light bathed the landscape and increased the visibility from black silhouettes to muted colours.

Dark blue gradually gave way to light blue and the eastern sky took on a mixture of white, yellow, pink and orange. After almost an hour, as a thin orange line, the edge of the rising sun appeared over the horizon next to one of the distant city towers. Within about five minutes, the line grew into a large, bright orange circle climbing alongside the tower and bathing the nearby rocks in a special pink hue. In another five minutes, as the remarkable orange sphere rose, it looked smaller but ever brighter. Its light was now giving the surroundings their full colours.

For the next six hours or so, the sun will continue its journey upwards with ever-increasing brightness and warmth. The buildings, trees, and rock formations will form shadows in its path, providing a welcome relief from the desert heat. Around noon, the sun will slowly start a downward journey toward the west. In another six hours or so, with fading brightness and a remaining fire-like glow, the orange sphere will dip behind the horizon, painting the western sky with light blue, pink and yellow hues. It will soon thereafter appear on the other side of the earth where life will begin for another day.

With the sun having set, the daylight fades and the distinct silence of night descends. The sky gradually turns navy blue to black with myriads of stars gradually appearing. The moon may soon, or perhaps later, rise from behind the horizon in one of its phases between a thin crescent and a circle. After another twelve hours or so of darkness, the whole cycle will repeat itself, separating one day from the next.

What is in a day? Divided into two main parts – light and darkness, or day and night – there are 24 hours in it, or 1,440 minutes, or 86,400 seconds. Within this time period, without fail or interruption, the earth moves around its own axis and exposes most of its surface to the sun for varying number of hours. The parts of a day – sunrise, morning, noon, afternoon, sunset, and night – all evoke certain moods and feelings. We may ponder about the rhythm of life and our part in the universe. What is the significance in all this?

Where did the day come from? According to the biblical story in the book of Genesis, at a specific point in the past, God created the sun, moon and stars to separate the day (light) and night (darkness), to give light to the earth, and to mark days, seasons and years.[1] While this description of origins is not intended as an exact historical or scientific account, it expresses in the beauty of poetic language the reality that surrounds us and points to a transcendent ground of all being.

Light and Vision

Each day consists of a period of light and darkness. Light is a tiny part of an immense, mostly humanly invisible, electromagnetic radiation spectrum consisting of an enormous range of frequencies. More specifically, light is only the very small part of radiant energy from the spectrum that is visible to human eyes. For many decades, physicists used two models for explaining the nature of light – a particle model and a wave model. It has now been confirmed

---

[1] Genesis 1:3-5, 14-18

that light indeed has the characteristics of both, sometimes behaving like particles and sometimes as waves. The quantum theory attempts to reconcile these two phenomena – light behaves as a wave but comes in tiny energy packages, or quanta.

The sun is the main source of natural light on the planet. (When the sun is not shining, people have harnessed the natural phenomena of fire and electricity to light up their environment.) Light is essential for the life of most earthly organisms with the exception of certain microorganisms and deep sea life. Without sunlight there would be no vegetation, no oxygen production through photosynthesis, and hence no life as we know it.

Light reveals characteristics of objects, aids to their understanding, magnifies their beauty, and raises appreciation of them. Compare a spring meadow or a still mountain lake seen at noon on a clear day with seeing it before daybreak or at dusk. Notice the difference between sunlit flowers with those in the shade. Light also cheers the soul. We instinctively feel better on a sunny day than on a gloomy, cloudy one when the sun's light is obscured.

Light in visible and invisible forms pervades the universe and connects us to outer space. The light we perceive from the myriads of stars in the night sky has travelled at a speed of about 300,000 kilometres per second, 18 million kilometres per minute, or one billion kilometres per hour over eons of time to reach us. So the light we see today left a distant star millions or billions of years ago. Using powerful telescopes to see or photograph faraway galaxies, astronomers can give us a glimpse of what the universe was like in a long-ago past closer to its beginning. So in a sense, light is a means to travel back in time over otherwise insurmountable distances.

In the non-physical realm, light symbolizes knowledge, understanding and education. The 14th to 16th centuries of the Renaissance, following the Middle Ages, were characterized by a rebirth of art, culture, music, and intellectual thought. The mid-seventeenth to mid-nineteenth centuries became known as the Enlightenment period – the age of rationality, science and technology, when the scientific method, reason, and logic came to the fore. Humankind began to discover the secrets of their world through observation, scientific experimentation, and travel. Since that time, knowledge and understanding in numerous areas, including astronomy, physics, biology, psychology, genetics and medicine, have increased almost exponentially, resulting in highly advanced technological developments.

The marvels and intricacies of the human body have been better grasped. Medical science has progressed in eliminating certain diseases. Education in hygiene and healthy lifestyle, contributing to the prevention of illness, is commonplace in the Western world.

Remarkable communication devices, ranging from the printing press to the phone, fax, radio, TV, computer, and satellite, exist to disseminate knowledge and information. From our living rooms we can view what is happening on the opposite side of the planet. We can also talk to and even see someone at the other end of the earth. High-speed trains and airplanes enable us to scale thousands of miles in a matter of hours. And photographs taken through powerful telescopes can give us awesome glimpses of outer space.

In the spiritual realm, beyond concepts and reason, light symbolizes truth, goodness, virtue, and ultimately God. While the peoples in ancient cultures worshipped the sun, intuitively recognizing it as the source of light, life and goodness, the biblical record reveals God as the true light and the ultimate source of life, truth and goodness. Then, if there is a Creator God, it would seem logical that knowledge about successful living would start with this transcendent giver of life. Also, if light represents truth, righteousness and God, darkness would symbolize falsehood, wrongdoing, and an evil one, represented in the Holy Scriptures as Satan the devil.[2]

Even though darkness can portray evil, the night sky also pictures divine glory and majesty. The magnificence of the myriads of stars, nebulae, constellations, and galaxies – only visible against a dark background – is awesome. While humans can see only a tiny fraction of the total incomprehensible reality, the presence of transcendent goodness and grace can be perceived even in dark situations – both literally and figuratively – for those who have eyes to see. As light, albeit mostly invisible, pervades the entire universe in the form of energy and radiation, the transcendent divinity – represented in the New Testament as triune God (existing in three forms) – is also omnipresent as life-giving and life-sustaining energy without which nothing would exist.[3]

Darkness can also be a symbol for the divine mystery, the nothingness (no-thing-ness) of the divine realm. Looking up to the starlit sky, we are reminded of the awesome unfathomable that surrounds us and of which we are a part. The root meaning of the word "mystery" is to shut one's eyes

---

[2] Psalm 27:1; Micah 7:8; Luke 1:78-79; John 8:12; 12:46; Acts 26:16-18; 2 Corinthians 4:6; Ephesians 5:8

[3] Psalms 19:1-4; Romans 1:18-21; Exodus 20:21; Isaiah 45:3, 7; Amos 4:13; Psalm 139:7-16; Nehemiah 9:6; Colossians 1:15-16; Hebrews 1:3

and ears. Mystery is silence, darkness. The night calls us to set aside time away from the busy demands of the day and to connect with that dark but grace-filled mystery in which we are immersed.

Darkness and Blindness

While advances in knowledge and understanding have benefited humanity, contentment and meaning in life still escape many. Also, interpersonal and international conflicts, as well as oppression, discrimination, war, disease and poverty continue. Just as most of the light spectrum is invisible to human eyes, a large amount of knowledge, both physical and spiritual, remains out of human reach – people are blind to it. Consequently, much darkness persists on the earth and in people's minds. Without divinely revealed light and truth accessible through the heart and intuition rather than the mind and reason, humans walk in darkness and experience problems, suffering and death.[4]

The Scriptures relate how in history God revealed himself in special ways to Abraham, Isaac, and Jacob. To their descendants, the nation of Israel, he gave a law with many principles for a physical life of joy and peace. Through the nation Israel – the descendants of

---

[4] 1 Corinthians 8:1-2; 13:8-12; Job 36:26; Romans 11:33-34; Deuteronomy 29:29; Isaiah 60:2; Hosea 4:6-7, 14

Jacob that later separated into two kingdoms, Israel and Judah – God preserved what have become the Old Testament scriptures.

Later, the Divine entered time and space through the God-man, Jesus Christ, to reveal previously unknown information about God – but only some had the eyes to see it. During his earthly ministry, Jesus magnified the Old Testament teachings, set a perfect example, and introduced the way to salvation. He was the true Light, opening the door to divine love, peace, joy and purpose – even in the midst of suffering, conflict, and apparent hopelessness. This is the real enlightenment that is available to humans only through the Holy Spirit – which is part of the divine light.[5]

Jesus Christ's followers recorded his life story and amplified his teachings in what we know as the New Testament. It, together with the Old Testament, has become recognized as the inspired Word of God, the Holy Bible. Those who reject divine revelation and testimony inevitably find themselves groping and stumbling like the blind and yet never realizing their true condition. Darkness and blindness are the same

---

[5] Acts 7:2-50; John 1:1-5, 9-13; 3:19-21; 8:12; 9:5; 12:46; 14:6; 1 John 1:1-2

in their effect. In the dark, there is no difference between the blind and the seeing.[6]

Interestingly, a prominent aspect of Jesus' work while on the earth was to give sight to the blind. While he did this dramatically in the physical realm, sometimes he also did it, less obviously, in the spiritual realm – by giving people perception of spiritual knowledge and enabling them to believe. In some cases, the physically blind received both physical and spiritual sight. In other cases, only spiritual sight through illumination of the mind needed to be given. At times spiritual light was rejected – the people preferred to remain in darkness.[7]

Since humanity tends to ignore divine revelation, much of the world lies in darkness, under the sway of an evil one that the Scriptures describe as the devil, the ruler of this world, who has blinded and deceived it. Sometimes what the world considers as enlightenment can actually be half-truths, distortions, or lies. While the evil one and those associated with him pose as light-bringers, they are in reality deceitful.[8]

---

[6] Isaiah 59:9-15; Proverbs 4:19; John 11:9-10; Romans 1:21-24; Matthew 15:13-14; 23:16-24
[7] Luke 4:18; Matthew 9:27-30; 11:4-5; 12:22; 15:30-31; 21:14; John 9:1-41; 12:40; Acts 28:23-27
[8] Romans 5:21; Ephesians 4:17-19; John 3:19; 2 Corinthians 4:4; Revelation 12:9; 2 Corinthians 11:13-15

Even the historical Enlightenment period, while bringing increased understanding of the created order, was ironically a time when research and science began to dismiss divine revelation and wisdom gained through the heart and intuition from beyond the mind and reason as valid or reliable sources of truth. As people turned to their own ways, they introduced new paradigms of morality and ethics, sowing seeds of relativism, amorality, and ultimately, immorality. This has resulted in a harvest of family breakdowns, rebellion toward authority, violent crime, and other evils.[9]

Spiritually, many people are like a person born blind, walking in darkness without being aware of it or knowing what they are missing. In what can only be described as a mystery and miracle, after Christ's death, resurrection, and ascension to heaven, as well as at other times in the history of humanity, the Divine has drawn and called out from the world individuals into the way of light. Just as God separated light from darkness at the beginning, his light is pushing away darkness from the hearts and minds of many. Those that perceive this drawing and respond to the call are convicted, inspired, and empowered to do the will of God and be a light in the dark world. As they seek to walk more closely with the Divine, the

---

[9] Proverbs 22:8; Hosea 8:7; Galatians 6:7-8; 2 Timothy 3:1-5

light of their example increases and shines ever brighter. Through their lives of love, kindness, and good deeds, God is glorified.[10]

Light and darkness – good and evil – are opposed to each other and remain incompatible. There is an unceasing struggle between them. Those who begin to be receptive to the light of God find that in their minds the darkness of deception fights against the recognition of the light and truth. The New Testament, containing the words of Jesus and his followers, exhorts to alertness and watchfulness – being on guard against temptation, deception, and thoughts leading us astray. The metaphor of being children of light is used as the day is a time when we have light, are awake, active, and can go about our work. By contrast, the night is a time of sleep and unconsciousness. It is also characteristically when evil is committed – when drunkenness, stealing, and other vices occur under the cover of darkness.[11]

With the help of divine power – the Holy Spirit – the mind and heart become more and more open to light. As a result, darkness is pushed out little by little

---

[10] Acts 13:47-48; Ephesians 1:11-14; 4:1-4; ; 2 Corinthians 4:6; 1 Thessalonians 5:4-8; 2 Timothy 1:8-10; 1 Peter 2:9-12; Matthew 5:14-16

[11] Romans 7:14-8:1; Matthew 24:42-44; 1Timothy 4:16; 1 Peter 5:8-10; 1 Thessalonians 5:2-7; John 9:4; Ephesians 5:8-11; James 1:13-15; 2 Corinthians 10:5-6

till eventually it will be all but eliminated. Light has the power to drive out darkness – darkness cannot resist the invasion of light, it can only seize the place of light when the latter gives way.[12]

In the biblical narrative of the book of Exodus, God used darkness as part of the frightful judgment poured out on Egypt before Israel's deliverance. The Old Testament prophets, as well as the apostle John in the apocalyptic (highly symbolic) book of Revelation, indicate that in the last days, before the prophesied return of Jesus Christ, darkness will again descend on the earth during a cataclysmic time of judgment.[13]

However, in contrast to the unprecedented days of trouble and anguish prior to Christ's return to earth, a time is coming when darkness will be totally banished. The apostle John and others describe this as a time when there will be no more night, no more sin, no more deception, no more evil ones, and no more suffering. The light and knowledge of God will fill the earth as the seas cover its surface. Destruction, war and conflict will have disappeared forever. The glory of God will make even the sun and moon unnecessary – the brilliance of the triune Divine will be the

---

[12] 2 Corinthians 6:14-18; Galatians 5:17; Ephesians 6:12; James 4:4-8; Romans 7:7-23
[13] Exodus 10:21-23; Isaiah 13:9-11; Jeremiah 4:22-28; Amos 5:18-20; Revelation 16:10

unceasing light of the new heaven and the new earth – a place of happiness without bounds.[14]

Different Views of Life

The day from sunrise to nightfall can portray the progression of physical life from birth to death. As the day is born with the sun coming up to the horizon providing only little light and warmth, we are born with little strength.

Like the growing and brightening sun reaching its highest point in the sky, we grow and develop to a peak in our physical life. Again, as the day declines with the sun on its journey west, our life declines physically as we reach our "sunset years". Late afternoon and sunset often have special beauty. The same can be true of one's senior years. While physical energy and strength are abating, there is beauty as a result of acquired maturity, wisdom, and spiritual insights.

For those who believe in multiple rebirths during one's existence, each new day can picture a fresh beginning – a new life with opportunities for doing better than the last time.

The Old Testament scriptures suggest that a day starts in the evening, at sunset.[15] A period of dusk or

---

[14] Zechariah 14:6-9; Isaiah 11:1-9; 60:18-22; Revelation 21:3-4; 23-27; 22:5

twilight is followed by the darkness of night. Dawn then comes with gradually increasing brightness. This movement in a day can be seen as picturing human physical existence followed by an afterlife – a fleeting temporary life, death, resurrection, and a glorious eternal spirit life.

Like the brief dusk period with its limited light, human life is short and passing – at most only nine or ten decades, and often much less. In contrast to eternity, the Scriptures compare this life to a mist, grass, a flower, or a fleeting shadow. Also, we live in a world where we will always only understand in part – a dimly illuminated twilight world.[16]

By the end of a day, we grow weary and look forward to a rest. The night's sleep can picture the death that all humanity is subject to as a result of having chosen to go contrary to the divine light. In sleep, there is inactivity and unconsciousness of what is happening in the surrounding environment. On many occasions, the Word of God portrays death as a sleep with no activity or thoughts. The Old Testament describes the dead as knowing nothing, unable to

---

[15] Genesis 1:5; Leviticus 23:32; Nehemiah 13:19
[16] James 4:13-15; Psalm 39:4-5; 90:5-6; 102:11; 103:15-16; 144:4; Job 14:1-2; 1 John 3:2; 1 Corinthians 13:9-12

praise God, and powerless to make plans or partake in any activities of the living.[17]

Dawn pictures a new day, an awakening to eternal life – time when light replaces darkness and goodness replaces evil. One prophet of old referred to Jesus as "the Sun of righteousness". He will usher in a day that will last forever. Those who have walked with the Divine during their physical lives will then know God fully. All questions and mysteries will be progressively unlocked and understood – in a new era full of light, characterized by no night, no pain, and no death.[18]

The dawn can also represent hope. After each dark night, morning always arrives – the sun always rises. Therefore in due time, life's dark nights – times of crisis, struggles, and intense suffering – too will pass.

A breaking new day can likewise picture a person being led into more and more understanding of spiritual realities – having been called from death and darkness to life and light. Little by little we learn about God and divine purposes, and begin to perceive wonderful things in inspired writings and in the world around, since God is in all things.

---

[17] Hebrews 9:27; John 11:11-14; Luke 8:49-56; 1 Thessalonians 4:13-15; Ecclesiastes 9:5-6; Psalm 6:5; 115:7; 146:4; Isaiah 38:18-19

[18] Malachi 4:2; 2 Peter 3:13; Daniel 12:2,13; 1 Corinthians 15:18-23; 51-54; 1 Corinthians 13:12; Revelation 21:3-5

Each new day can be a reminder that we have already experienced a spiritual resurrection by being enlightened and enlivened by the Holy Spirit. Even now, we already have dwelling within us the seed and promise of eternal life. While the outer body is unchanged or deteriorating, the inner person has been and continues to be renewed – having become a new creation in Christ. We have died with Christ to our old way of life with its selfish desires and pursuits and been raised with him to walk in newness – being transformed into his image and following his example of love and kindness.[19]

As the sun rises and shines ever brighter, we may be able to visualize the risen Jesus Christ in his splendour and remember the promise that one day we will see him as he is and be like him.[20]

---

[19] Ephesians 2:1-6; John 3:36; 5:24; 2 Corinthians 5:17-21; Colossians 2:20; 3:9-10; 2 Corinthians 3:18
[20] Matthew 17:2; Revelation 1:12-16; 1 John 3:2

All in a Week

Up at 5 am, take a meditation walk in the crisp morning air, a quick bite for breakfast, get dressed, and out the door to catch the 6:30 bus to work. The third copier has been out of order for the last few days and the male repairman cannot come into the female section of the building till after all the women have left for the day – by which time he is ready to go home himself. I surely hope I can get my handouts duplicated before class.

With somewhat unmotivated students to teach, the day has its challenges and stresses at the best of times. Then the boss comes into the office and asks how Sara is doing. Her mother was wondering why she got a D for English writing last semester. Sara can hardly string sentences together, so a D on her report was really a gift of grace. Yet her mother is complaining.

The kids always complain about something. Usually it is quite trivial or ridiculous, and being a private school depending on parental financial support, the administration has to tread carefully. The teachers are the ones that get squeezed between a rock and a hard place.

This is what the week can look like for a foreign teacher of English in a strict Muslim country. After five days, the need for a break becomes urgent!

In our Western society, it is more and more common for people to feel the necessity to work seven days a week. Their company may be understaffed for the demands and expectations of the bosses, and all the projects don't get done in a 40-hour week. Others may need to put in overtime to meet their monthly expenses – otherwise the pay runs out before the next one is due.

Yet, taking a day out for a change of pace after a stressful week is refreshing and health-conducive. A day to sleep in – even catch up on sleep missed due to late nights and early mornings; a relaxing breakfast – maybe take the family out for brunch; a walk in nature with time to stop and take in the beauty of the blossoming acacia bushes visited by bees, or discover among the leaves a bug with an interesting pattern on its back; perhaps visit a place of worship or enjoy coffee and cake with likeminded friends.

Weekly Rest Day in History and the Bible

Historically, religious traditions have instituted a weekly day of rest and spiritual rejuvenation. For the Jews, based on the Old Testament writings, it is the seventh-day Sabbath or Saturday. For most Christians it has become Sunday, the day of Jesus' resurrection. For the Muslims, it is Friday. Whatever the day, it has kept in the minds of believers a consciousness of a divine transcendent reality in whatever way they understand it, and it has also given them a sense of community and identity. The Jews, for instance, scattered all over the world, would not have survived as a distinct group if it wasn't for the Sabbath binding them together.

No astronomical phenomenon exists for a week like there is for the day, month and year. According to the biblical narrative of creation, the seven-day weekly cycle started with God having worked six days at bringing the world into existence and then setting aside the seventh day as a time of rest. While the six-day creation account in the book of Genesis is metaphorical and not intended as a scientific or literal description of origins, helpful principles for human life emerge. They include the importance of balance of work and rest and between the physical and spiritual aspects of life.[21] While this chapter interprets a weekly day of rest from the biblical perspective, those of other persuasions may find the metaphors applicable to their lives as well.

Seven-Day Cycles in the Bible

In Bible symbolism, the number six pertains to humans and their activities. Humankind is said to have been created on the sixth day and given six days to do their work. Time, into which we have been placed, is divided into hours, minutes, and seconds – all multiples of six.

By contrast, the number seven is used in the Scriptures to denote divine work of completeness or perfection. For example, the seventh day, on which God rested and which was later set aside for his people as blessed and holy, symbolizes God's work of a completed physical creation. In the context of the Flood, representing divine judgment, Noah was checking every seven days to see if the waters had subsided. In the apocalyptic, largely symbolic, writings of the book of Revelation, the number seven features prominently in end-time events before Jesus Christ's return to the earth.[22]

---

[21] Genesis 1:1-31; 2:2-3; Exodus 16:23; 20:8-11
[22] Genesis 1:24-31, 2:1-3; Genesis 7:4,10; 8:10-12; Revelation 5:1; 8:2, 6; 13:18; 15:1; 16:1

Seven-day intervals also figure prominently in Israel's history in connection with divine laws or activities. For example, sick people were quarantined for seven days at a time and ordination of priests took seven days.[23] The annual God-ordained festivals of Unleavened Bread and Tabernacles were observed for seven days.[24] There was a seven-day period that the Israelites circled Jericho till on the last day, the city's walls miraculously fell through divine power. Also, in the days of King Ahab of Israel, God granted his people victory over Syria after a seven-day standoff by the opposing armies.[25]

Sabbath as a Rest Day

The six-day work week and seventh-day Sabbath rest was an important landmark for ancient Israel. God instituted the Sabbath for his people on their way from Egypt to Mount Sinai, making it a sign of a special covenant with them. It then became one of the Ten Commandments. In addition to commemorating the creation of the world, the Sabbath was a memorial of Israel's redemption and delivery from the Egyptian slavery. It was also a sign of their being set apart (sanctified) and God's ownership over them.

---

[23] Leviticus 13:2-6, 21, 26-27, 31-34; Exodus 29:29-30, 35; Leviticus 8:31-35

[24] Exodus 12:15-19; 13:6-7; Leviticus 23:6; 34-42

[25] Joshua 6:3-16; Hebrews 11:30; 1 Kings 20:28-29

The Sabbath kept God in the memory of Israel. When they departed from observing the Sabbath, they also lost sight of God and resorted to idolatry. With increasing spiritual and moral corruption came divine judgment, and finally the people were exiled out of their land to Babylon.[26]

During his earthly ministry, Jesus Christ transformed Sabbath-keeping as understood by the Jews of his day – the descendants of those who returned to Palestine after the exile. Fearful of another divine judgment, the law-enforcing Pharisees wanted to keep the people safe by instituting hundreds of Sabbath regulations. Ironically, this made the Sabbath into a burden and bondage, rather than the intended rest and liberation.

Proclaiming himself the "Lord of the Sabbath", Jesus showed how love, mercy, and compassion should supersede strict Sabbath observance. Also, his ministry of teaching, healing, and providing for human needs was fulfilling what the Sabbath typified – bringing rest and alleviating suffering which points to the eternal rest of the saved state where all suffering ceases. Upon Jesus' death, the new covenant was inaugurated and the old covenant with the laws of Moses became obsolete. These ancient laws and

---

[26] Exodus 16:22-26; 20:8-11; 31:12-17; Deuteronomy 5:12-15; Ezekiel 20:10-24; 2 Chronicles 36:15-21

requirements were shadows pointing to higher spiritual realities introduced by Jesus Christ and accomplished through the Holy Spirit.[27]

Spiritual Realities Depicted by the Sabbath

As biblical Israel was delivered from Egyptian bondage and became the people of God, we have been delivered from the bondage of sin and death, and are now a new creation in Christ. We have been redeemed through the shed blood of Jesus on the cross. Analogous to the exodus from Egypt and the wilderness journey to the Promised Land under the leadership of Moses, we are on a journey to a glorious destination under the leadership of Jesus Christ.[28]

The Sabbath as ancient Israel's rest day is also a symbol of the righteousness by faith through the rest in Christ. While we are to consciously practice goodness and grow in love and virtue, we do not need to overcome our shortcomings solely on our own strength. Understanding that trying to earn salvation by obedience to the law is impossible, we can accept Christ's sacrifice as a means of our forgiveness and justification. As we surrender to God and enter the

---

[27] Matthew 11:28-30; 12:1-8; Mark 2:27; Hebrews 4:1-11; 8:8-13; Colossians 2:16-17

[28] Romans 6:14; 7:5-6, 25; 8:1-2; Ephesians 2:1-5; Galatians 4:3-5; John 8:34; 2 Corinthians 5:17; 1 Peter 1:18

rest in Christ, he does the work of imputing and imparting his own righteousness from within, through the Holy Spirit. Rather than attempting to win God's favour by our efforts, our obedience expresses love and gratitude for what Jesus Christ has done on our behalf. We are being made into new persons, being saved, and being given true rest, both now and in its fullness in God's kingdom. The result of this transforming work is a life of virtue (holiness or sanctification).[29]

While a minority of Christians believes that the seventh day (Saturday) of the Ten Commandments should still be observed, most others over the centuries have made Sunday – the day on which Jesus Christ rose from the dead – a day of remembering their Lord.[30] They have carried over to it the principles of physical rest and spiritual rejuvenation. However, in today's fast-paced world, not many allow themselves to take a whole day for rest and spiritual pursuits. A correlation may be seen between this and increased incidence of stress, burnout, lack of faith, doubt about spiritual realities, and other problems.

The weekly observance of a day of rest can be a time of physical and spiritual refreshment, as well as of sharpening one's perspective on life. Such practice

---

[29] Romans 3:20-28; 5:9; 12:2; 1 Corinthians 6:11; 2 Corinthians 3:18; Ephesians 1:7; Hebrews 13:12
[30] Mark 16:9; Hebrews 4:4

would also contribute to a balanced life of work, rest and recreation, which is conducive to physical, mental and spiritual health. A day set apart to seek God is comparable to ascending a mountain or a lookout tower from which the heavenly "Promised Land" or eternal rest can be glimpsed each week between the sometimes arduous stretches of the "wilderness journey" of work and other day-to-day concerns. During this time, we can "spy out the land" to which we are going and be reminded of the divine promises.[31]

In summary, the Sabbath concept (adapted to one's own culture and tradition) can be regarded as a symbol of delivery and liberation from oppression, stress, disease, and other suffering resulting from the human condition; consciousness of a transcendent reality (the Divine, Source, ground of all being, etc.); and the ultimate joyful rest in the new heaven and new earth (nirvana, paradise, and so on) with freedom from all pain, suffering, death and sorrow.[32]

---

[31] Numbers 14:6-8; Deuteronomy 2:7; 8:2; Hebrews 11:8-10, 13-16

[32] Revelation 7:17; 21:3-4; 22:3; Isaiah 35:9-10

All in a Month

Not long after the sun had set and the lighter blue sky gave way to darkness, a soft glow appeared among the trees in the east. A few minutes later, the large yellow orb of a full moon came into view, bathing the whole area in a delicate light. As it rose, it became smaller but brighter. On a clear night, the full moon light dims the glory of the stars and gives sufficient light to see objects and to find one's way around. On such nights my husband and I often take a walk in a nearby park. Sometimes we stop at the lake edge and admire the moon's reflection in the still water. Other times we may pause on the little bridge, gaze at the moon, and reminisce of a time several years ago when a life-changing turning point occured in our lives on a full-moon night in July.

Lunar Phases and Life Cycles

In a *lunar* month, the moon orbits the earth approximately every 29.5 days. During that time it passes through a cyclical pattern. At the beginning of the month, the new moon is barely visible as a thin crescent in the sky. Day by day it grows in size and a week or so later, about half of the moon is visible from the earth. Mid month, the full moon appears, with its full splendour lasting only three or four days before it starts diminishing. By the end of another week, it is only half visible again, and by the end of the fourth week the cycle starts once more with a new moon.

The silvery moon has always been a source of enchantment. In late summer, the so called harvest moon appears extra large and bright and has helped reapers working late to get their crops in. In Islamic countries, sighting the new moon is the sign that the holy month of Ramadan, when Muslims fast during the daylight hours, has officially started or ended.

The moon phases can be compared to the cycle of life – a small beginning, growth toward a peak, and a slow decline. These phases may also be seen as denoting beginnings, culminations, turning points, and declines in various life situations as well as in history. Civilizations, empires, nations, and companies have gone through such cycles. Yet, with every decline and end, there is always the hope of a new beginning. Death, or the end of something, carries with it the potential of a rebirth or a new start.

Moon Phases in Biblical Israel

The calendar months of ancient Israel, referred to in the Old Testament, were based on the moon phases, as well as tied to the seasons and harvests of the year. The continued correspondence with the seasons was achieved by adding a thirteenth month seven times in 19 years, which made the Hebrew calendar *luni-solar*. (Some of the world's calendars, such as the Islamic one, are based purely on the moon phases and hence are not tied to the seasons.) Each month started with a new moon and was marked by special worship. The first day of the first month, corresponding to March-April or spring in the northern hemisphere, was for Israel the beginning of the sacred year.[33]

In the first month (Hebrew *Abib*) and seventh month (Hebrew *Tishri*), special festivals occurred either on the new moon or the full moon. The Feast of Trumpets (Jewish *Rosh Hashanah*) was kept on the first day of the seventh month – a new moon. The Passover and the First Day of Unleavened Bread were kept on the fourteenth and fifteenth day of the first month – a full moon. The beginning of the Feast of Tabernacles (Jewish *Sukkoth*) was on the fifteenth day of the seventh month – also a full moon. Pente-

---

[33] Numbers 10:10; 28:11-14; 2 Chronicles 8:12-13; Ezekiel 46:3; Amos 8:4-5; Exodus 12:2

cost (referred to as the Feast of Weeks in the Old Testament) and the Day of Atonement (Jewish *Yom Kippur*) fell between the new moon and full moon.[34] Orthodox Jews are still observing these festivals. The Feast of Trumpets (Jewish *Rosh Hashanah*) marks the start of the civil year.

Based on related scriptures, the Feast of Trumpets, a new-moon festival, may be seen as foreshadowing Jesus Christ's second coming to the earth, the nearness and fruition of which will be heralded by a literal or figurative trumpet sound.[35] The Messiah's return will be a dramatic turning point and a new beginning in world history. Scriptures refer to this period as the Day of the Lord or Day of God. It is also portrayed as a day of darkness, clouds and gloominess, war and slaughter, and judgment.[36] In contrast, for the people of God, it is a day of resurrection to eternal life – also a turning point and a new beginning in a glorified and immortal existence.[37]

It has been suggested that Jesus' birth or first coming – another dramatic event in the history of

---

[34] Leviticus 23:23-25, 5-8, 34-39; 15-16; 27-32
[35] Isaiah 27:13; Zechariah 9:14; Matthew 24:31; 1 Corinthians 15:22; 1 Thessalonians 4:14-17; Revelation 8:2-10:7; 11:15-18
[36] Isaiah 13:9-13; Jeremiah 46:10; Ezekiel 30:2-3; Zephaniah 1:14-18; Revelation 16:14
[37] Daniel 12:1-3; 1 Corinthians 15:22-23, 50-54; 1 Thessalonians 4:13-17; 5:8-10

Israel and humankind – also occurred at the time of the Feast of Trumpets, rather than on the traditionally observed December date. While this cannot be conclusively proven, certain biblical facts give support to the idea. Shepherds were keeping their flocks in the fields – December would have been too cold to do this in Palestine. A bright star appeared to herald Christ's birth – suggesting a dark night rather than a full-moon night. Christ's ministry started when he was about thirty and ended after three and a half years – in the middle of the first month, at Passover time.[38]

The full-moon festivals also point to climactic events. Passover and Unleavened Bread bring to remembrance the Exodus – God's deliverance of Israel from Egypt's Pharaoh and grinding slavery. In its New Testament parallel and fulfilment, Jesus Christ, through his death, has delivered spiritual Israel, the church, from Satan and the power of death which enslaves all of us in fear. He inaugurated the new covenant and opened the way into the kingdom of God through forgiveness and reconciliation. Humans now have the opportunity to become children of

---

[38] Matthew 2:1-2, 9; Luke 2:8-20; 3:23; John 18:28-32, 39-40

God.[39] Jesus has also delivered each person turning to him from the slavery and penalty of sin.[40]

The Feast of Tabernacles, the last festival of the Israelite year, started at the time of the full moon and was a celebration of the main harvest. Some believe that when Jesus Christ returns, he and the immortal saints will rule on earth for a thousand years (or an indeterminate period), teaching humanity the ways of God. The festival could be seen as pointing to this period.[41] Another way of viewing this ancient harvest celebration is as the great harvest (typifying salvation) of all humanity. This is in contrast to the small first-fruit harvest commemorated during the spring and early summer festivals of Passover and Pentecost.[42]

God's kingdom over the earth is described as a time when the divine way of life will fill the earth, Satan will be forever banished, and all deception will come to an end. Wars, sickness, suffering, crying and death will be things of the past. The new earth, where God dwells with his people, will be full of light. Neither the sun nor the moon will be needed. With

---

[39] Exodus 12:6-17, 21; John 1:10-13; Ephesians 1:3-14; 2:14-22; 3:1-6; Hebrews 2:14-15; 8:10-13; 10:16-20

[40] Romans 6:6-7, 11-14, 17-23; 1 Corinthians 5:6-8

[41] Revelation 20:1-6, Zechariah 14:16-21

[42] Exodus 23:16; 34:22; Matthew 9:35-38; 13:36-43; Revelation 14:15-16

God being fully and totally all and in all, the climax of God's plan of salvation will have been accomplished. But while we wait and look forward to this wonderful consummation, each month the changing moon in the sky can keep renewing our hope.[43]

---

[43] Isaiah 2:2-5; 11:6-10; Zechariah 14:5-9; 1 Corinthians 15:24-28; Revelation 21:1-5; 22:1-6

All in a Year

 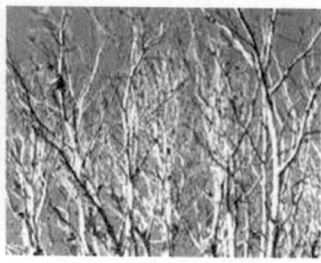

What a year it has been for our family and friends! This time last year, we came back from Europe hoping to settle in the new home we had just purchased. But job search in Australia proved difficult and it became obvious that we had to go and teach overseas – this time in Asia. Through a set of amazing circumstances, teaching positions opened up for both of us in Choenan, South Korea. We had barely known the name of the capital, let alone where Choenan was. Now we are here – in a very foreign culture, unable to read signs on shops, and surrounded by people speaking an incomprehensible language, yet kind and eager to help in their broken English.

In the same year our friends had twins after ten years of trying and all but losing hope of conceiving. Another friend's teenage daughter was tragically killed in a car accident – and emotionally her mother died with her. Our niece Evelyn got married and went to live in Latvia. Our nephew Carl and his partner had a baby boy to the delight of the new grandparents. Aunt Sylvia lost her husband to cancer after only five months since he was diagnosed with the disease. Uncle Jim and Aunt Ali divorced. Uncle Paul had a stroke and now his wife needs to care for him. Aunt Frances found out she had Parkinson's disease. And Uncle John lost his wife in a devastating flash flood.

The world at large has also had a turbulent year. Financial turmoil, earthquakes in several areas, destructive fires in other regions, an oil spill devastating a pristine shoreline and its ecosystem, floods, draughts, civil wars, and more. Multiple thousands died in natural or man-made disasters, armed conflicts, or famines.

A year can bring major changes – both good and bad into our lives. Situations can change from being single to getting married, from married life to divorce or widowhood, from being a couple to becoming a family, from health to terminal illness or disability. We may find ourselves in a new area, new job, or a new unexpected situation that we couldn't have planned, foreseen or prepared for.

Seasons of the Year

A year is roughly the time it takes the earth to circle the sun on an elliptical (though nearly circular) path. This annual orbit, taking about 365 days, creates different seasons and weather patterns around the world. In equatorial areas, warm seasons only vary in the amount of rainfall. In the polar regions, daylight ranges from 24 hours a day to no daylight. The temperate zones of the earth have four seasons – spring, summer, autumn and winter. These annual seasons can picture both human life on earth and God's eternal plan for humanity as portrayed in the Holy Scriptures.

As the stories above illustrate, one's individual world or the world at large can undergo a major transformation in a year – as if from winter to spring and summer or in reverse. Some lives may transition from one extreme to the other like the polar regions. Other individuals' lives seem to be more on an even keel – similar to the tropical regions. However, just as weather is not fully predictable and seasons come and go, our life situations too are impermanent and can turn in unexpected directions. But there is always hope that even after a long, dark winter, eventually the sun will return – sometimes in the nick of time.

This essay focuses on the four seasons in temperate regions showing how each season can typify a stage in life and besides its challenges can also have much beauty.

Spring

Spring is a time of new beginnings – indeed a time of rebirth or resurrection in nature. What seemed dead suddenly shows signs of life. With the sun's warming rays, growth and a flurry of activities resume after the cold deadness of winter. Shoots and buds appear, soon turning into leaves and flowers. Animals produce offspring and start nurturing the young. With its newness of life, this may be the loveliest time of the year.

In physical life, spring reflects birth and youth. It is a time of rapid growth – the change from a tiny bud to a leaf or flower, for example, seems phenomenal and takes place almost overnight. Likewise, a newborn baby grows, develops, and learns faster in its first year than at any other time in life.

Similarly in the spiritual life, spring pictures a new birth and life – the change that takes place in conversion. New Testament texts show that before conversion, non-believers are "dead in sins" and separated from God. With the new birth they receive new life and are now empowered to live for God.[44] A thus

---

[44] John 3:3-8; 1 Peter 1:23; Ephesians 2:1, 4-7, 11-13; 4:20-21; Romans 6:1-14; 2 Corinthians 5:17-19

transformed individual who has been "born of the Spirit" excitedly learns about God, hungers for the divine way of life, and obeys God no matter what the cost. The Scriptures caution against losing this excitement, growth, and "first love". [45]

The winter to spring transition can be seen as the change to take place in the resurrection – a glorious metamorphosis from death to eternal life, from corruption to incorruption, from mortality to immortality. As trees shed their dry leaves, appear dead for a time, and then return to life in the spring, so too the human body ages and dies, but will yet come back to life in a future resurrection.[46]

Spring is also a time when nature clothes itself with greenery. Lush meadows replace seemingly dead winter grass and deciduous trees become attired with new bright green foliage. Clothes in the Bible symbolize virtue, while rags or nakedness portray unrighteousness.[47] As God clothes the grass, flowers and trees without any effort of their own, so he attires his people in righteousness – by grace, since salvation cannot be earned by human effort.[48]

---

[45] Acts 2:44-47; 4:32-37; Matthew 24:12-13; Galatians 6:9-10; Philippians 2:12-13; Hebrews 12:3-4; Revelation 2:4-5

[46] 1 Corinthians 15:35-54

[47] Job 29:14; Isaiah 64:6; Zechariah 3:3-5; Revelation 3:4-5, 17-18; 6:9-11; 16:15; 19:8-9, 14

[48] Matthew 6:28-30; 22:9-11; Luke 24:49; Romans 13:14; Ephesians 2:8-10

Late spring (and early summer) is a period of maturing and bearing fruit. The small early harvest at this time of year depicts a young person growing into adulthood and beginning to contribute to the lives of others. In biblical metaphor, the virtuous are compared to fruitful trees, whereas the unrighteous are likened to fruitless, dead, or uprooted trees. The people of ancient Israel were to be a fruitful vineyard for God, but history shows they failed. Similarly, the people of God today are called to produce good fruit through Jesus Christ, the vine that they are a part of. Spiritual fruit such as love, peace, kindness and self-control is evidence of the Holy Spirit working in a person's life.[49]

Summer

Summer is typically a pleasant time – a season with bright sunshine and warm temperatures. With its long days, early sunrises, late sunsets, and extra energy, it is also a productive time. Nevertheless, continuous hot and humid or very hot and dry days can be enervating and tiring. In some areas, summer can also be a time of violent weather, such as hurricanes, typhoons, excessive rains and flooding. In summer time, crops ripen and become ready for

---

[49] Psalm 1:1-6; 52:8; 92:12; Isaiah 5:1-7; Jude 1:10-12; Matthew 7:15-20; John 15:1-8; Galatians 5:22-25

harvest. Trees are forming fruit – attractive to behold and eagerly anticipated for its flavourful nutrition. Young animals are growing up and being taught survival skills.

In human life, summer can picture early adulthood to middle age – a time of marriage, child bearing, bringing up children, and engaging in a productive career. Spiritually, it can be seen as a season for maturing – enjoying the new life in the Spirit, but also being disciplined and purified through tests and trials. Difficulties can include marriage problems, the challenging teenage years of growing children, unexpected illness, job loss, and financial losses.

Autumn

Autumn is associated with welcome cooling from the summer heat and a season when in dry areas the earth receives rain. In temperate regions, it is the time of year that is visually past its best. Signs of aging are everywhere. The beauty of new life has disappeared, and adorable young animals have grown up and lost their special cuteness. Nonetheless, this season has its own beauty – such as in the changing colours of deciduous trees ranging from yellow to orange to red to brown. The autumn is also time to harvest ripe, delicious fruit and express gratitude with rejoicing over God's goodness.

The autumn of human life is likewise a time past one's physical best. The reproductive capacity ceases, strength and energy diminish, and wrinkles and gray hair become unmistakable evidence of getting older. To compensate however, "a harvest" of children and grandchildren may be a blessing from God. Furthermore, the fruit of the Holy Spirit is often more evident than before – love, peace, joy, patience, goodness – accompanied by godly wisdom gained through the years of walking with God.[50]

Winter

Late autumn and early winter portray old age and death. As with the unstoppable process of dead leaves falling from trees, so in human life family members and friends inevitably pass away. Aging can be a difficult time of loss, sorrow, health problems, and the awareness of one's own approaching death. However, both nature and God's Word give hope that this is not the end. Spring always follows winter – there is always a more encouraging time to look forward to.

In nature, some animals survive the winter in hibernation. This can be paralleled with the biblical metaphor of sleep used to refer to human death.[51] The

---

[50] Psalm 127:3-5; 128:3-6; Proverbs 2:6; 16:31; 17:6; Galatians 5:22-25; James 1:5

[51] Matthew 9:23-25; John 11:11-15; Acts 7:60; 13:36; 1 Corinthians 11:30; 15:20

Scriptures then point to a time of resurrection and new life. As the spring with its warm sun starts a new cycle of life, so Jesus Christ, the "Sun of righteousness", will return to bring new life to those who have died.[52]

Seasonal Celebrations in Ancient Israel

A large part of the Old Testament is a story of Israel, the descendants of the patriarch Jacob, later renamed Israel. The nation's worship is tied to the annual seasons and can be instructive even to us living in the 21st century.

Under their covenant with God, ancient Israelites were required to observe three Holy Day seasons – falling in spring/early summer and in the autumn. These seasons corresponded to two harvests – an early small harvest (firstfruits), and a later large harvest. Two rainy seasons occurred that helped to bring the harvests to fruition.[53]

Biblically speaking, harvests are symbolic of conversions, ministering to the saved, and bringing people into God's kingdom. Timely rain is one of God's blessings and a vital agent in producing a good harvest. In the Scriptures, rain may be analogous to

---

[52] Malachi 4:2; Daniel 12:2-3; 1 Corinthians 15:51-54; 1 Thessalonians 4:13-17
[53] Deuteronomy 16:16; Exodus 23:14-16; Joel 2:23-24

God's teachings and the Holy Spirit, the means of conversion and salvation.[54]

The first festival period, in the spring, was the Passover followed by seven Days of Unleavened Bread. On the Sunday during this festival time, a sheaf of the first fruits of the harvest was presented to God. This ceremony typified and looked forward to Jesus Christ, who later became the first of the firstfruits. He was the first to be resurrected, glorified, and accepted by the Father on the Sunday after his crucifixion.[55]

Seven weeks after the firstfruits offering came the Feast of Weeks – referred to in the New Testament as Pentecost – during which two leavened bread loaves were offered to God. On the first New Testament Pentecost, the Holy Spirit descended, writing God's law on fleshly hearts (in contrast to tables of stone as occurred on Mount Sinai). On that day, 3000 were converted in a dramatic way – the first members, or firstfruits, of the church founded on the apostles and the prophets with Jesus Christ being the chief corner stone.[56]

---

[54] Matthew 9:35-38; 13:37-43; Luke 10:1-2; John 4:34-38; Revelation 14:15; Leviticus 26:4; Isaiah 44:3-5; 55:10-11
[55] Leviticus 23:4-11; John 20:1-17; 1 Corinthians 15:20-23; Acts 26:23; Colossians 1:18
[56] Leviticus 23:15-17; Acts 2:1-41; 2 Corinthians 3:3-18; Ephesians 2:19-22

The last major festival in ancient Israel was the Feast of Tabernacles, celebrated after the ingathering of the main autumn harvest. Based on the harvest typology, together with other indications in Scripture, it can be postulated that there is yet a large future harvest of the saved.[57]

Paradise – Old and New

Written in a metaphorical style, the first three chapters of the book of Genesis describe an ideal setting and conditions for earth's first humans. They were placed in a paradise, named the Garden of Eden with the tree of life, a symbol of immortality, freely available. However, after the first couple chose to go contrary to God's instructions, they brought upon themselves and their descendants the penalty of death. Their disobedience to the Creator resulted in curses on humankind and the whole creation.[58]

At the end of the Bible, the book of Revelation describes paradise restored. The tree of life is again freely available, and curses, pain, suffering and death are gone forever. A river of the water of life, lined with trees of life in multiple varieties, flows through the Holy City. The perpetual glorious light of God

---

[57] John 6:44, 65; Romans 8:22-23, 28-30; Revelation 20:1-6; 12-15; Ezekiel 37:1-14; Romans 11:25-32

[58] Genesis 2:8-9, 15-17; 3:14-19; Romans 8:19-23

makes the sun, moon and lamps unnecessary. There are no more nights and no more seasons. However, harvests never cease as the trees provide different life-giving fruit every month. While the sun, moon and seasons have their beauty and even inspire awe, something better could yet be in store for humanity and the whole universe. Like the best wine brought forth toward the end of the wedding feast in Cana, God may have kept the best for last.[59]

---

[59] Revelation 21:1-8, 23-27; 22:1-5; John 2:9-10

Little by Little

Slowly, almost imperceptibly, the night gave way to another day. When we left the house to take a walk in the early morning coolness, it was still dark. Gradually, the stars grew dimmer and the eastern sky turned a lighter blue. Silhouettes became visible objects and a new day dawned. Birds greeted the day with chirping. Before long, the sun rose from behind the hilly horizon and bathed the surroundings in its golden rays. Flowers that had closed for the night began to slowly open in response. Nocturnal creatures such as bats, hedgehogs, owls and foxes retired till evening, when the day slowly gives way to night – and the cycle of night and day repeats itself.

Universal Law of Gradual Change

One of the universal laws of nature is gradual progression. Many things around us change, for either better or worse, little by little. Differences, invisible minute by minute or even day by day, become noticeable over a period of time.

Seasons in temperate areas gradually change from winter to spring to summer to autumn, and back to winter. Temperatures slowly increase as the year advances towards spring and summer – perhaps by one degree every week. By a minute or two each day, the daylight period gets longer and the nights become shorter. The reverse occurs in moving from summer to autumn and winter.

Likewise, weather often changes little by little. A coming storm may only appear as a few scattered dark clouds on the distant horizon and a slightly rising wind. Thunder may be faintly heard in the distance and lightning seen from far away, but slowly they move closer and closer. Morning fog lifts bit by bit to reveal a blue sky, sunshine, and possibly a breathtaking view. Falling snow descends quietly and gently, first in tiny clumps of individual flakes, gradually increasing to a heavier fall. After a time, a winter wonderland emerges as the ground becomes covered in a majestic white robe.

Growth and development in the animate world also proceeds little by little. Life itself arose through a long-time progression from one stage into another – an evolutionary process estimated to have taken billions of years. Flowers blossom, trees bud, leaves appear, then tiny fruit, which slowly grows and ripens till harvest time. Infants develop through a number of stages into adulthood. Children progressively learn to crawl, walk, run, speak, read and write. They also acquire habits and develop socially, morally and spiritually.

Like growth, decay and decomposition is also a gradual process. Vegetable matter on the compost pile undetectably turns into rich dark soil. The possum electrocuted on the power line and fallen to the ground slowly decomposes and disappears, the seemingly invisible process aided by insects, worms and microorganisms. A disease or illness may start almost unnoticeably with mild symptoms which slowly worsen. (Healing works gradually in the opposite way.) Nations and empires, having reached their peak, decline economically and morally, often imperceptibly from a day-to-day perspective. All these transitions from one state to another are a function of time, and progress almost undiscernibly while we watch.

Gentle Working of the Divine

In a similar manner, God has often worked with humankind in a gradual and gentle way. God's kingdom of grace entered barely noticed with Jesus Christ's first coming into the world. A humble birth took place in an ordinary family, in an insignificant town, in a stable outside a crowded inn. It was acknowledged only by a few shepherds and a handful of Persian astrologers who saw an unusual star. Immediately thereafter, the family became fugitives, fleeing from their country to protect the baby's life from the infanticide directive of a jealous king. The one named Immanuel ("God with us") grew up in Nazareth, a small town of no repute. His miracles, including healings, were misunderstood and judged to be of the devil. Finally, revealing his identity led him to a cruel death by crucifixion. Yet, in all of this progression of seemingly insignificant events, God's incredible purpose was accomplished. Christ's love was demonstrated and he was glorified. The seeds of the church were sown, ready to sprout, grow, and gradually spread around the world.[60]

The Bible reveals God as gracious, kind, and slow to anger. Through the Messiah, God has opened the way to salvation and draws, appeals to, and reasons with those whose ears are open to his calling. He waits patiently for them to come to him, to acknowledge their shortcomings, and to recognize their need for a deliverer from their human condition – always giving them time and in love honouring individual freedom of choice. Elijah found that God spoke

---

[60] Luke 2:1-20; Matthew 2:1-16; Mark 3:1-6; 6:1-6; 15:21-37; Acts 2:1-41

to him not loudly and dramatically – not in a whirlwind that ripped through and scattered the rocks where he was, not in the earthquake and fire that followed – but in a still, small voice.[61]

The forbearing, patient and gentle approach can, unfortunately, lead people to delay or neglect turning to God. If not careful, even believers can lull themselves into a lethargic or spiritually drowsy state. Since evil deeds are not immediately punished, warnings often fall on deaf ears. Deception and a false sense of security easily set in. "Things have always been this way," many claim. Others may say, "Preachers have talked about end times for centuries. Wars, diseases, and famines have always been around, so what is new? Given time and knowledge, humanity will solve their problems."[62]

God's kingdom has broken into this world and through the global availability of the gospel message is spreading slowly but surely. Evil is also gradually increasing and permeating societies while the fullness of God's reign is awaited. Although much of humanity has chosen to reject or ignore their Creator and sceptics abound, God is nevertheless not mocked. Cause and effect laws – sowing and reaping – are operating quietly, almost imperceptibly, behind the

---

[61] Nehemiah 9:17-25; Acts 3:19; 17:30-34; 26:20; 1 Kings 19:11-13
[62] Ecclesiastes 8:11-13; Revelation 3:14-17; 2 Peter 3:3-7

scenes. As a consequence of human actions, wars, famines and disease epidemics are on the increase. So are, and not always in a gradual, gentle way, floods, earthquakes, tsunamis, hurricanes, and other natural disasters. In times of the resultant human distress, consciousness of the divine may be heightened and God can work in such situations for his ultimate glory.[63]

When Little by Little Doesn't Work

The Scriptures predict a time at which the world will have reached a point when without divine intervention humankind would destroy the planet and themselves. Then, God will no longer delay but send his glorified Son Jesus to the earth for the second time – not as a humble, gentle, self-sacrificing servant, but as a triumphant King of kings. Christ's coming is described as being preceded and accompanied by dramatic cataclysmic events that will put unspeakable terror into human hearts and cause unprecedented death and destruction.[64]

In this period of gentle grace, the Bible lovingly warns us to be vigilant, and to remain faithful to our God, thereby being ready for his kingdom. The

---

[63] Matthew 24:6-7, 12-14; Colossians 1:6, 23; Galatians 6:7-9; Romans 1:18-32

[64] Matthew 24:21-22, 29-30; Luke 21:25-27; 2 Peter 3:10-12; Revelation 6:12-17; 16:17-21; 17:14; 19:11-21

Scriptures do not reveal when Jesus will return. Nevertheless, the end of life is for each person the time of meeting their Saviour. May all of us, while we have time and opportunity, be on guard against the gradual moral and spiritual decay around us, hear and respond to the still small voice of God, and submit to the loving Father who in incredible love and grace offered his Son for the salvation of humankind.[65]

---

[65] Mark 13:33-37; 1 Peter 5:8-10; 2 Corinthians 2:11; Matthew 24:42-44; 25:13;1 Thessalonians 5:1-6; John 3:16

Turning Points

"One small step for man, one giant leap for mankind." Some have personally watched as it was happening, and many have since viewed documentary footage from July 1969 as American Neil Armstrong, one of the Apollo 11 astronauts, first put his foot on the surface of the moon. A historical moment, it was a turning point for the United States as far as the space race with the former USSR was concerned. It was also a life-changing spiritual experience for those involved. Awed by the event, Armstrong quoted from Psalm 8 in the Bible: "When I consider your heavens, the work of your fingers, the moon and the stars, which you have set in place, what is man that you are mindful of him, the son of man that you care for him?"[66]

Seven months before the historic moon landing, at Christmas time 1968, the earth inhabitants saw for the first time how their planet looks from 350,000

---

[66] Psalm 8:3-4

kilometres away. As the Apollo 8 crew orbited the moon, they photographed the "earthrise". Viewing the blue planet from outer space, they were moved to quote the story of creation found in Genesis 1:1: "In the beginning, God created the heavens and the earth...."

On earth that Christmas, especially in the United States, people were touched and inspired. It was a memorable end to a hard and turbulent year that saw political unrest on several continents, a number of coup d'états, and in America growing protests against the Vietnam War and the discrimination of blacks. Americans also witnessed the assassinations of the Civil Rights leader, Martin Luther King and of the presidential hopeful for that year, Senator Robert F. Kennedy.

The present generation well remembers September 11, 2001, when two hijacked airliners destroyed the New York World Trade Center twin towers. The event quickly made it into history books around the globe. The world, being plunged into a global war on terrorism, has not been the same since.

All of us carry in memory moments or events that have become turning points in our lives. Some are joyous or triumphant, such as a wedding day, the birth of a first child, or a long-desired milestone reached. By contrast, shocking and tragic events also confront us from time to time, for example, an accident, an act of violence, or an untimely death. Both types of events can take us beyond ourselves into the mystery of life and make us awed or raise some soul-searching questions.

Turning Points in Biblical History

Throughout history, special incidents or occurrences becoming turning points can be seen in retrospect. Some may have seen insignificant at the time they occurred. Consider, for example, the drunken orgy of the Babylonian leadership and nobility, which enabled the astonishing Persian takeover and resulted in a change of dominating empires.[67] Among the more dramatic consequences would belong a decree of the Persian king, Cyrus, commissioning the Jewish exiles to return from Babylon to their homeland and to rebuild Jerusalem and God's temple (around 458 BCE). This marked the beginning of a prophesied "69 weeks" or 483 years before the arrival on earth of the Messiah, Jesus Christ. Later, around 336 BCE, an ambitious young Macedonian, Alexander the Great, with a vision to conquer the world defeated the Persians and became the head of the next empire.[68]

---

[67] Daniel 5:1-31
[68] Ezra 1:1-4; Daniel 9:24-27; 8:20-22; 11:2-4

According to the biblical narrative of Genesis, God allowed an evil being, Satan the devil, to enter paradise. Disguised as a serpent, one of God's good creatures, and using subtlety and deception, Satan lured the recently created humans away from allegiance to their Creator. This event radically changed the course of human history. Not unlike a time bomb planted by a terrorist, Satan's influence soon brought about suffering, destruction, and death. An explosion of evil and violence started with the fratricide of Adam and Eve's second son and culminated in a universal corruption of the human race. This brought judgment and destruction to the whole earth.[69] However, it was not to be the end of the story – only a turning point and interlude to accomplish a greater purpose that the sovereign God had decreed in eternity past.[70]

Almost 2000 years before Neil Armstrong stepped on the moon, God's Son, Jesus Christ, arrived on the earth. He did not come in a computer-guided spaceship, and the event was not telecast to the then civilized world. Rather, he came humbly as a helpless baby born to a young Jewish girl from an insignificant background; being delivered not in a well-

---

[69] Genesis 3:1-24; 4:3-8; 6:5-14; 7:21-24
[70] Genesis 3:15; 1 Peter 1:18-20

equipped hospital, but in an animal shelter outside an overbooked Bethlehem inn.[71]

From the general populace, almost no one noticed or cared. Certainly no hero's welcome, except by heavenly angelic hosts who knew what was happening and praised God. Only a few local shepherds, after being told by an angel what had taken place, believed, went to see, glorified God, and spread the news. Later, a small group of wise men from the East understood that a king had been born and came to worship him with gifts. In contrast, the ruling king, Herod, wanted no competition and sought to kill the child.[72]

This seemingly insignificant event – the tiny segment of timeless eternity when Jesus Christ entered time and space, and humanly speaking, lived and died as a failure – is one of the most important events ever, and a dramatic turning point in human history and future. Yet even today, some are still unaware of it, let alone understanding its significance. In a sense, it was a divine declaration of a war on terror – terror by the devil, the universal deceiver, destroyer, and murderer whose instigations and activities from the

---

[71] Luke 2:1-7
[72] Luke 2:8-20; Matthew 2:1-14

beginning of human history have left billions killed, maimed and grieving.[73]

While it may not yet be obvious, the heavenly war on terror has been won. The Son of God, fully divine and fully human, has conquered Satan, defeated death, and pioneered the way to eternal life for all who will respond to him. Even though on the surface there seems to be little change, Satan's days are numbered, and like leaven in dough, the kingdom of God is slowly and steadily spreading on the earth.[74]

Upcoming Turning Points

In earth's future, another special event and universal turning point is destined to occur. The same God-man, Jesus Christ, who was killed but vanquished death, will again step on our planet. His return, however, will not be quiet and go unnoticed. The New Testament portrays Christ coming as a conquering King of kings, his arrival accompanied by piercing trumpet blasts and loud shouts of angels. A momentous, spectacular, unprecedented occasion, it will leave no one unaware – every eye will see him, not unlike people watching Neil Armstrong step onto the moon. Not all will cheer and welcome him,

---

[73] John 8:44; 10:10; Ephesians 2:2-3; 6:12-13; Job 1:12-19; 2:7
[74] Matthew 13:33; Colossians 2:13-15; Hebrews 2:14-15; 2 Timothy 1:10; 1 John 3:8; Revelation 12:7-12

however. While those who have waited for him will have their expectations fulfilled and rejoice, others will be terrified and seek death.[75]

The Word of God also reveals what is humanly incomprehensible at this time – yet in some way these ancient promises will be fulfilled. Those who have the Holy Spirit working in them and are alive at Christ's coming will be changed in the twinkling of an eye from mortal to immortal. This will be preceded by a resurrection of the just. Countless people who have been dead for years, decades, centuries, or millennia are to rise to life and receive glorious bodies in an unfathomably special moment. They will see the glorified Lord face to face and have his likeness.[76]

The Bible leaves readers with glimpses of other special times and turning points lying yet in the future. All creation is to be liberated from the abuse and bondage it has been subjected to for so long. There will be a new heaven and new earth, the home of virtue and justice. All evil, including Satan and his cohorts, will be banished, and there will be no more deception, hate, fighting, killing, wars, disease, or suffering. Finally, God will come to earth for the rest of eternity to dwell with redeemed humanity – those

---

[75] Matthew 16:27; 24:30-31; Acts 1:11; 1 Thessalonians 4:16-18; Revelation 1:7; 6:16-17; 19:11-21; 22:7, 12, 20

[76] Daniel 12:1-3; Romans 8:9-11; 1 Corinthians 15:42-57; 1 John 3:2

who will have responded to the divine offer of life everlasting and become the children of God through a supernatural birth from above. [77] What glorious time is ahead consisting of undreamt special moments without parallel!

---

[77] Romans 8:19-23; 2 Peter 3:13; John 1:12-13; Revelation 5:9-14; 20:6-21:7

Time for Everything

Even with patches of snow on the ground in our Czech village and the surrounding fields, spring was undoubtedly in the air. The brighter sun and longer days together with opening snow flowers and crocuses were unmistakable signs. Before too long, the apple and cherry trees would burst into bloom making the orchard spectacularly beautiful. The stork would return to her old nest on top of the factory chimney and Mr. Hulka, our octogenarian neighbour who had observed the stork's return for decades, would remark that spring has definitely arrived.

Around April, the first swallows will be sighted. They will have made a hazardous ten-thousand-kilometre journey from Africa to Central Europe, crossing mountains, seas and deserts in four to six weeks. The birds who miraculously didn't succumb to starvation, exhaustion, storms and other perils will start building new mud nests or return to their old nests to lay eggs.

One can't help but wonder: How do the plants and trees know when to start budding and blossoming? How do the birds and other animals determine when to set out on their migratory journeys?

Time-Based Universe

Ours is a clockwork universe where everything is governed by time. The earth's movement on its axis results in day and night; the moon's revolution around the earth determines the month length; and the earth going around the sun marks a year and creates seasons. Interestingly, the biblical creation account records: "And God said, 'Let there be lights in the expanse of the sky to separate the day from the night, and let them serve as signs to mark seasons and days and years, and let them be lights in the expanse of the sky to give light on the earth.' And it was so."[78]

Nations and societies have developed various instruments to measure time. Calendars are used to count days, months and years, all based on the movements of heavenly bodies. In modern times, the Western countries use the solar Gregorian calendar; the Muslims have a lunar calendar which doesn't keep pace with the seasons; and the Chinese and Hebrew calendars are luni-solar, making adjustments for the seasons by periodically inserting additional

---

[78] Genesis 1:14-18

time. In the case of the Hebrew calendar, for example, an extra month is added seven times in 19 years. Calendars have also been constructed based on the movements of certain stars.

From the earliest human history, people have observed the periodicity, or regular recurrence, in the geophysical world, as well as in the physiological and behavioural cycles of living organisms. Associated with the rising and setting of the sun, the waxing and waning of the moon, and the annual changes of seasons are other patterns. These include tidal movements, seasonal appearances and disappearances of plants, migrations of birds, waking and sleeping patterns, menstrual cycles, and reproduction. A definite connection exists between the biological and geophysical cycles.

To be able to live in harmony with the daily, monthly and seasonal rhythms of nature, all living things in the plant and animal kingdoms have internal biological clocks. These physiological timers exist for almost every type of periodicity known, but the most observed and studied have been the circadian, or daily, rhythms. For a short time, circadian rhythms can work independently of external cues such as sunrise and sunset, showing that they are internally programmed. However, to continue working accurately over a long time, they are automatically reset by environmental cues given by the movements of the earth, moon and sun. Light is the most common of these prompts, known as _zeitgebers_ (from German meaning "time-givers").

A physiological timer appears to involve two systems at work – a *master clock* or pacemaker found in the brain, and *local clocks* located in the body's various organs. The master clock, which is reset by light entering light receptors in the retina and other environmental cues, synchronizes the local clocks. Furthermore, a molecular basis exists for the functioning of the biological clocks in that hormones play a role in sleep and wakefulness, metabolic rate, body temperature, and the corresponding behaviour. Also, specific genes, proteins, and biochemical mechanisms have been found to be responsible for circadian rhythms.

Internal clock mechanisms are responsible for such phenomena as Siberian hamsters and other mammals in northern regions changing their brown summer coat colour to white for the winter, bears going into winter hibernation, and swallows flocking together in preparation for their autumn journey to Africa. The mechanisms also send humpback whales on their seasonal migrations between the equator and the North or South Pole. Likewise, salmon, before the end of their lives, make their one and last journey upstream to where they hatched to lay eggs for the preservation of the species. The signs of aging are thought to result from the various body clocks gradually getting out of synchronization with the master clock in the brain.

Sovereign Time Master

In addition to the astronomical and biological clocks, the Scriptures reveal a sovereign Time Master who rules the universe and governs the time therein. The supreme Mind behind all that exists transcends time and space but has designed and engineered all the other clocks and keeps them running.

The Word of God shows that God has even determined the destiny of nations as well as when, for how long, and where individuals would live.[79] In divine timing, therefore, empires rise and fall, rulers come and go, and prophesied events take place to fulfil eternal plans and purposes.[80] From individual promises to national and global promises, they have come to pass "at the appointed time", "in due time", or "when the time was fulfilled".[81] Other predicted events have not yet come to pass, but with eyes of

---

[79] Acts 17:26; Deuteronomy 32:8; Job 12:23; Psalm 102:23-24; 139:16; Proverbs 16:9
[80] Nehemiah 9:24; Job 12:17-25; Psalm 135:8-12; Daniel 2:21; Mark 1:15
[81] Genesis 17:21; 18:14; 21:1-2; Daniel 11:27-35; Romans 5:6; 9:9; Galatians 4:4-5; 1 Timothy 2:5-6; 6:13-16

faith, one can have hope that they will yet be fulfilled – at the right time.

A key predicted event is the return of Jesus Christ to the earth.[82] While for some events, such as the end of the Babylonian captivity, succession of certain empires, and even Jesus' first coming to the earth, a time was given, we do not know the time of Christ's second coming. With this uncertainty, we are exhorted to be ready at all times.[83] Believers in all generations, from the first-century original apostles to now, have expected Jesus to return in their time. And, in a way, he has. The Bible teaches that the next instant of awareness for those who died in faith will be in Christ's presence. For the rest of us, time is not yet fulfilled, but in due course it will be as well.[84]

The writer of the Old Testament book of Ecclesiastes aptly states: "There is a time for everything, and a season for every activity under heaven."[85] Ultimately, humans are subject to divinely appointed times and changes beyond their control – God has sovereignly predetermined the overall course of history's events. Even some key occurrences in individual lives may be destined to happen – though free

---

[82] John 14:1-3; Acts 1:10-11; Matthew 24:30-31; Revelation 1:7
[83] Jeremiah 25:8-14; 29:4-14; Daniel 9:25-27; 11:2-45; Acts 1:6-9; Matthew 24:36-44
[84] Philippians 1:21-26; 1 Thessalonians 4:13-17; 2 Peter 3:3-4,8-13
[85] Ecclesiastes 3:1

choice has a significant part to play and there is a mysterious interaction between divine will and our free will.

Either way, much that happens to us, and even the timing of what we desire and plan, is beyond our control. Achieving greater peace in life lies in the acceptance and appreciation of divine guidance and perfect timing.

In the Nick of Time

Near perfect weather conditions existed the morning that Mike with his wife and three young children (as well as their four native assistants) set out on the last leg of their boat journey in returning from their missionary assignment in Papua for a welcome break at home. The glory of the day, however, belied the unexpected tragedy that would soon follow.

As Mike turned the boat's ignition key, a blinding explosion rocked the boat and enveloped it in flames. Suffering burns and other injuries, everyone jumped into the water and with what strength they had, struggled to swim ashore. Traumatized by the experience, with some in the group not being good swimmers, a life-and-death drama in the crocodile infested river followed. Clinging together and helping each other, miraculously, all except one of the children made it to shore. The ordeal was not over, however. Desperately needing medical help, they had to yet face a two-day gruelling canoe trip. Almost despairing of life, they finally arrived at a settlement where none too early a doctor was available to assist them.

Everyone has heard dramatic stories, where timing made a difference between life and death. Miners trapped underground, earthquake survivors buried under collapsed buildings, skiers caught in an avalanche, hikers lost in a mountain blizzard, and critically ill or injured persons receiving last-minute emergency assistance. Many times, rescue came in the nick of time and was the key to survival.

Critical Timing in Nature

Nature itself has built-in instances of critical timing. Animal life cycles sometimes involve situations where time is of the essence for successful continuation of the species.

The Antarctic emperor penguin females, for example, have barely enough time and energy to mate, lay an egg, transfer it to the male for incubation, and make a 50 to 80 kilometre journey on foot from the breeding grounds to the sea to feed before their internal food reserves are depleted.

Some whales do not eat while migrating and feeding their calves en route. If they don't reach the distant feeding grounds in time, exhaustion or starvation puts their life at risk. Migratory birds likewise fly across oceans without eating and must reach their destination before their energy runs out.

Certain insect species have just a limited window of time to establish the next generation and thus preserve their species. After 13 or 17 years underground in the nymph stage, periodical cicadas emerge by the millions, all at the same time, in eastern parts of North America. They only live about 30 days, during which time they need to mate and lay eggs.

Among the fish, the Pacific salmon undertake a long, arduous journey from the sea to the river of their origin. Once out of the ocean and in the river, they stop feeding and travel relentlessly upstream for weeks, sometimes hundreds of kilometres and over great obstacles. Bruised, battered and travel-worn, with their last remaining energy they spawn. Creating a suitable nest, the female lays thousands of eggs, which the male fertilizes and the female then covers with gravel. Having secured offspring, the adults die only a few days later.

Last-Minute Divine Intervention

The Scriptures recount numerous stories where in the face of danger, disaster or death, God intervened in the nick of time. In Sodom, angels rescued Lot in the last minute from an angry mob and from perishing in the destruction of the city. In faith and trust, the patriarch Abraham prepared to sacrifice his only child as commanded, believing that God could and would raise him from the dead to fulfil the divine promise. Instead, God dramatically intervened at the last moment, stopping Abraham from killing the boy and providing a lamb instead.[86]

When the Israelites left Egypt, the mighty Egyptian army pursued and rapidly caught up with them. Only God's nick-of-time intervention of spectacularly opening the Red Sea spared the people from disaster. Some, such as Hezekiah in the Old Testament and Epaphroditus in the New Testament, would have died of an illness unless God had intervened in the last minute. In his missionary endeavours, the apostle Paul reached a point of despairing of life in the face of danger and hardship, yet God strengthened and spared him.[87]

Believers have remarked that God is seldom early, but never late. What may seem from the human perspective way overdue is often within God's perfect timing.

Even when God does not spare us from an unpleasant situation or fiery trial, all is not lost. The Bible shows that God may miraculously intervene within the circumstances. Daniel was not spared from being cast into a den of lions for his faithfulness to

---

[86] Genesis 19:4-11, 15-25; 15:4-5; 17:2-7; 18:10-14; 22:1-18; Hebrews 11:17-19

[87] Exodus 14; 2 Kings 20:1-6; Isaiah 38:1-8; Philippians 2:25-30; 2 Corinthians 1:8-10

God. While among the ravenous wild beasts, he was however supernaturally protected. His three friends were thrown into a blazing furnace, but likewise, miraculously shielded from harm. Instead, their determination to obey God regardless of consequences turned into a dramatic witness to the Babylonian and Persian kings and their assistants.[88]

When God Doesn't Intervene

Sometimes, in divine sovereignty, God may not act to prevent tragedy or disaster. However, after a time of learning – which can involve anguish and suffering – God may restore what had been lost. When the patriarch Job had lost property, family and health, he was later healed, given a new family, and acquired twice the previous possessions. Similarly, Mary and Martha suffered grief when their brother died of an illness. They then experienced a miracle superseding a healing when Jesus raised Lazarus from the dead.[89]

Biblical and personal testimonies of God having acted in the nick of time provide faith and hope. Nevertheless, the Scriptures and reality also show that deliverance may not always come in the way that we hope and desire. However, if rescue does not come, the Word of God reassures us that, even then,

---

[88] Daniel 3:1-30; 6:3-28
[89] Job 42:10-17; John 11:1-44

all is not lost. The heroes of faith who were not delivered in this life but died looked forward to a glorious future that was certain. We can too. [90]

---

[90] Hebrews 11:13-40

Strangers in Time

Sunset tinged the sky bright orange, then deep orange, fading into subdued hues of dark blue as the dusk and nightfall took over. The glory and inspiration of the experience, however, did not last long. Another day had ended. Day and night; new moon, crescent, half moon, full moon; spring, summer, autumn, winter – these all remind us of the cyclical passage of time.

Day after day, week after week, month after month, year after year, time flows like a river. Its current cannot be stopped and it carries us along with it – we move relentlessly from birth to death. Along the way we learn how to make the most out of this existence called life – a series of experiences in a small segment of time, compared in its shortness to a vapour, grass or flower.[91] Even though time governs everything, in some ways it is also incomprehensible

---

[91] Job 14:1-2; Psalm 103:15-16; James 1:10; 4:13-14; 1 Peter 1:23-25

– scientists don't fully understand the nature of time.

This journey through time can become stressful and difficult to cope with. The title of a 1960s musical and book, "Stop the World – I Want to Get Off", (said to have originated from a graffito) expresses the overwhelmed, helpless feeling of many in the Western world. Seemingly, there is no stopping, no exit, and no escape along the way – the only way out is death. In desperation, some tragically end their life by suicide.

Time is both an enemy and a friend. Inevitably it brings us closer to death. We change in travelling through time – growing, maturing and ageing. Time gradually robs us of our strength, vitality and cognition. Time brings to end beautiful moments. In the brief and fleeting nature of life, only memories remain when time has passed – a recording of experiences in our minds. But time also heals hurt, pain, sorrow and grief. Ideally, with the passage of time, we learn lessons, develop patience, build fortitude, acquire wisdom, and become kinder and more loving.

Divinity in Time

The sovereign God is both transcendent and immanent. Existing outside of our time frame, he is also involved in time, being present in all things. For about 33 years, God in Jesus Christ left the timeless dimension of eternity and entered time – leaving the divine and immortal realm of glory to become physical and mortal. (Yet, while on earth, Jesus was both divine and human – a mystery beyond rational or philosophical explanation.)[92]

God has also foretold future events and brought them to pass with timely precision. Types from the Old Testament were fulfilled in the New Testament on the exact day that symbolized them. For example, Jesus was crucified on the day in the yearly holy day cycle that the Passover lamb used to be slain. He rose and ascended to heaven on the day when the sheaf of the first harvested grain was waved before God on the Sunday during the Days of Unleavened Bread. The promised Holy Spirit came right on the day of Pentecost.[93]

The Jewish captivity in Babylon lasted 70 years, as foretold. Also, the events of the 70-week prophecy spanning the predicted period of 483 years between the Persian king's commission to rebuild Jerusalem and the beginning of Jesus' ministry were fulfilled on schedule.[94]

---

[92] John 1:1-4, 9-14
[93] John 19:14-18; 1 Corinthians 5:7; Leviticus 23:6-11; Mark 16:9; John 20:10-20; Acts 2:1-21
[94] Isaiah 48:3-7; Daniel 9:24-26 and Ezra 7:11; Jeremiah 25:11-12; 29:10; 2 Chronicles 36:21; Daniel 9:1-2

While God is active in time, he also exists beyond and outside of time in eternity. Divine existence is without beginning and end. Likewise, Jesus Christ as a member of the Trinity has no beginning or end of life, and the Holy Spirit is also eternal.[95]

By contrast, everything physical has a beginning and will have an end. The Scriptures refer to the beginning of time when the world, through divine creative power, came into existence. While we cannot be dogmatic about the when and how of physical origins – scientists are still trying to figure it out – it is an accepted understanding that there was a time when the present universe did not exist.[96]

Longing to Transcend Time

In the physical creation, humans are unique in having a consciousness of time and a sense of its dimensions – the past, present and future. They also comprehend their own beginning and inevitable end. At the same time, they desire to transcend death and to live on. Ancient civilizations, such as the Egyptians and others, provided abundantly for their dead in the hope and expectation of a life beyond death. The Scriptures reveal that God "has also set eternity in the

---

[95] Isaiah 40:28; 57:15; Hebrews 7:3; 9:14
[96] Genesis 1:1; Isaiah 40:21-22; 41:4; Matthew 24:21; Hebrews 1:10-12; 2 Peter 3:4

hearts of men" (Ecclesiastes 3:11). Deep inside, humans yearn for more than what the present life offers – restricted as it is to time and space.[97]

The good news is that God has made a provision to fulfil this transcendent longing. Through Jesus Christ's sinless life and sacrificial death, people can – upon accepting what the Saviour has done on their behalf – be reconciled with God who is the source of everlasting life. At Christ's return to earth they will be either resurrected or instantly changed to immortality – never again to suffer or die.[98]

On a Journey to Eternity

As we wait in time and space for the hope of eternal life to be fulfilled, we are already ambassadors and citizens of the heavenly kingdom. Therefore, our calling includes being lights to those around us – living and sharing the kingdom values of love, joy, peace and kindness. Being divinely empowered can help us be positive and productive – making the most of opportunities and using the time we have to develop talents and serve others. Rather than nostalgically looking back to "the good old days", we have a vision of a glorious future as we forge ahead – fol-

---

[97] Ecclesiastes 3:1- 2, 11; 9:3-5
[98] Acts 2:21-24, 32-38; Romans 2:7; 5:9-11; 8:10-11; 1 Corinthians 15:51-54; Revelation 21:1-5

lowing Jesus on our journey in time – toward timeless immortality.[99]

While in this time capsule, we are depicted by the Word of God as strangers and pilgrims on earth. Having embraced the values of the divine kingdom, we no longer fully fit into this world as we look forward to another time and dimension – referred to in the Bible as a heavenly country. Like the apostle Paul, we may long to leave the earth to be with Christ. However, God reveals himself through his activities and people in the world. As God's sons and daughters, we have the honour of representing our heavenly Father as his ambassadors through love and compassion toward fellow humans, whom God intends to also eventually transcend time and space.[100]

In God's sovereignty, as strangers in time, we may have each been put in a certain place, era and circumstances to fulfil a specific purpose for the divine kingdom – to serve God in a unique way in such a time as this. We can appreciate and rejoice in the good things of the physical creation – the lovely, pure and noble – and do what we can in our sphere of influence to make the world a better place. As we continue our journey, time brings us closer to when

---

[99] Ephesians 5:15-16; Colossians 4:5; Matthew 5:14-16; 25:14-46; Galatians 5:22-23; Philippians 3:8-14
[100] 2 Corinthians 5:20; Ephesians 2:19-20; Hebrews 11:9-16; 1 Peter 2:11-12; Philippians 1:21-26

we will transcend it and fulfil the longings of our hearts – to dwell in eternity with the glorious Creator who is all in all.[101]

---

[101] Philippians 4:8; 1 Thessalonians 5:16-18; Acts 17:26-28; Esther 4:14; Romans 13:11; 1 Thessalonians 4:13-17; 1 Corinthians 15:28; Revelation 21:3-5

About the Author

Eva Peck has a Christian and international background. Through Christian work as well as teaching English as a foreign language, she has experienced a range of cultures, customs, and environments. Having lived and worked in Australia, the United States, Europe, Asia, and the Middle East, she now draws on those experiences in her writing.

Eva refers to biblical passages in this book the way she has come to understand them. Having had the opportunity to fellowship with Christians from a variety of faith traditions, she however also recognizes that many faith-related issues can be understood in more than one way.

Eva studied both science and theology at the tertiary level, and has a Bachelors degree in biological sciences and a Masters degree in Theology. She lives in Brisbane, Australia, with her husband, Alexander. The Pecks' other books of spiritual nature include *Pathway to Life – through the Holy Scriptures* and

Journey to the Divine Within – through Silence, Stillness and Simplicity. Both publications, as well as their other books can be ordered online through www.pathway-publishing.org.

More About the Author's Other Books

Divine Reflections in Natural Phenomena

This book explores how spiritual realities can be glimpsed in the world of nature – in phenomena such as life and its order, the beauty and harmony around us, and the countless mysteries of the heaven and the earth.

Divine Reflections in Living Things

This volume looks at living organisms among both plants and animals and reflects on the glimpses of the divine in these realms. Readers are encouraged to pause and take a fresh look around them – to see each living creature and every process as if for the first time.

Divine Insights from Human Experience

This is a collection of writings drawn from the author's experience. Each piece begins with a story and is followed by reflections on the wisdom and/or spiritual insights gleaned from the various incidents. The book consists of two parts – *Wisdom from Life* and *Spiritual Analogies from Life*.

Pathway to Life – Through the Holy Scriptures

Pathway to Life presents in a concise and systematic way the basic teachings of the Bible. It strives to offer a balanced, nondenominational understanding of the Scriptures. Conclusions are supported by scripture references.

Journey to the Divine Within – Through Silence, Stillness and Simplicity

Journey to the Divine Within shares, through the reflections of a variety of spiritual writers, how to enter the realm of one's heart. One way that this occurs is through silence, stillness and simplicity. When pondered, the reflections will lead readers to the silence and stillness of their own hearts on the path to encountering the Life, Light and Love within.

Other Resources

Eva Peck has created several websites with spiritual content. Feel free to browse and explore.

Truth & Beauty
(www.truth-and-beauty.org)

This site seeks to capture what is true and lovely. With the aim of helping readers appreciate the nature of Ultimate Reality, it deals with practical and spiritual aspects of life. To uplift and edify, it provides galleries with beautiful nature images as well as heart-warming stories.

Pathway to Life
(www.pathway-to-life.org)

The site presents the essential Christian message under 36 biblical topics in Q & A style. Where several denominational views exist regarding a subject, these are covered as different interpretations. Supporting scriptures are given throughout. The information is also available in book form (see p. 106).

Heaven's Reflections
(www.heavens-reflections.org)

The site features the theme of seeing the extraordinary in the ordinary, the sacred in the daily, and the special in the routine. It focuses on how the world around us, upon deeper looking, reflects spiritual realities. This book, *Divine Reflections in Times and Seasons*, is based on the content of the website and is one of three on the same theme. The other two are *Divine Reflections in Natural Phenomena* and *Divine Reflections in Living Things*.

You may also enjoy visiting Alexander's websites:

Spirituality for Life
(www.spirituality-for-life.org)

The site shares information with the aim of presenting a practical spirituality to enhance one's life journey and to help fulfil one's divine destiny.

Prayer of the Heart – Journey to the Divine Within
(www.prayer-of-the-heart.org)

This site deals with the prayer of the heart, or meditation, covered from a mainly Christian perspective. It features quotations from a variety of spiritual writers. The content is also available in book form (see p. 107).

See also **www.pathway-publishing.org** for the Pecks' other creations.

Readers' Comments

I have finished reading the book *Divine Reflections in Times and Seasons* and have to say that it is excellent. I have found it educational, informative and at the same time easy to read. Each time I read one of your books, I am amazed at your knowledge. I have learned many interesting things and have also appreciated the spiritual side of the book. A book like this can be reread over and over.
Liba H., Capalaba, Australia

The section on paradise restored inspired me. Rather than nostalgically looking back to "the good old days", you point the reader to a vision of a glorious future. I note that you also acknowledge variety within Christianity saying "many faith-related issues can be understood in more than one way." ... Thanks for the great read!
Richard P., London, UK

The book, *Divine Reflections in Times and Seasons,* which "connects nature with spirituality" is a very easy and relaxing read for all, even people who regard themselves as "non-religious."

Eva takes the familiar in nature and time and compares it to spiritual realities with an abundance of scriptural references as footnotes. The small book can be comfortably read in one or two sittings, and the footnotes do not detract from the text.

Reading the book made me more reflective on the times and seasons going on around us every day. Eva weaves together the world of nature, astronomy and even the rise and fall of empires to illustrate the hand of God in time.

Nicholas P., Victoria, Australia

Thank you kindly for your book series *Divine Reflections*. I have skimmed through the previews and think that the books are indeed wonderful. I think that your work and words will be an inspiration to the many people that need them in this difficult world in which we are living. You have the experience, knowledge, ability and the spiritual background to reach out to people to give them hope. Well done!

Pauline G., Cairo, Egypt

Regarding your book, *Divine reflections in Times and Seasons*, your style of writing is very readable and sympathetic, and the way you reflect on the beauties of nature is lovely. Your message and discussion is soft and gentle and makes the reader feel God's love.

Margaret S., Thornlands, Australia

I found your book to be a blend of the cosmic Christ you have discovered in nature and the deep-rooted "word" which is imprinted in your heart.
Sadie M., Thornlands, Australia

The reflections on God's creation were delightful – it is so true, as the Bible tells us in Romans, that we can see the proof of the Creator in His handiwork all around us.
Jan H., Mittagong, Australia

About Pathway Publishing

Pathway Publishing is dedicated to sharing truth and beauty by publishing books that present what is true to life and reality, as well as what is lovely and inspirational. The goal is to not only provide sound information, but also to lift the human spirit.

Pathway Publishing has a vision of helping readers on their path of enlightenment and spiritual transformation. The wisdom and experience of spiritual teachers, thinkers, and visionary writers from various backgrounds and faith traditions are recognized and valued.

Other books produced by Pathway Publishing, beside the *Divine Reflections* trilogy, are:
- *Divine Insights from Human Life,* Eva Peck
- *Pathway to Life - Through the Holy Scriptures,* Eva and Alexander Peck
- *Journey to the Divine Within – Through Silence, Stillness and Simplicity,* Alexander and Eva Peck
- *Artistic Inspirations - Paintings of Jindrich Degen* arranged by Eva and Alexander Peck
- *Floral and Nature Art – Photography of Jindrich Degen* arranged by Eva and Alexander Peck
- *Memories of Times with Dad – Poems and Letters,* Alexander and Eva Peck
- *Volné verše,* Jindrich Degen (in Czech)
- Verše *pro dnešní dobu,* Jindrich Degen (in Czech)

Pathway Publishing

Seeking truth and beauty